The ASSIST Program

Affective/Social Skills: Instructional Strategies and Techniques

Helping Kids Handle Conflict:

Primary Version

A Validated Washington State Innovative Education Program

This publication is a product of the joint efforts of:

Pat Huggins

and

Lorraine Shakarian

SOPRIS WEST EDUCATIONAL SERVICES
A CAMBIUM LEARNING COMPANY

BOSTON, MA • NEW YORK, NY • LONGMONT, CO

Printed in the United States of America
08 07 06 05 04   06 05 04 03 02

Artwork by Ernie Hergenroeder & Dennis Tarenzio
Edited by Beverly Rokes
Layout by Sherri Rowe

ISBN #1-57035-200-3

Published and Distributed by

SOPRIS
WEST
EDUCATIONAL SERVICES

4093 Specialty Place • Longmont, CO 80504 • (303) 651-2829
www.sopriswest.com

18CON/BAN/6-04/.5M/976

Table of Contents

- ### *STEP 1: Stop*

   Students will learn to identify the cues in themselves and in others that signal an escalating conflict.

   Students will be introduced to a process they can use to de-escalate conflict.

   Students will learn and practice the self-calming techniques of "stopping" and "breathing" to de-escalate conflicts.

- ### *STEP 2: Think*

   Students will practice determining whether they should walk away or stay in a conflict situation.

- ### *STEP 3: Pick a Plan—Walk Away and Get Help From Someone You Trust, Do Something Else, or Cool Down*

   Students will learn to walk away and seek help from someone they trust, engage in another activity, or use an anger reduction strategy to avoid escalation of a conflict.

- ### *STEP 3: Pick a Plan—Stay and Ignore It or Say What You Want*

   Students will learn the strategies of ignoring a provocation and telling the provoker what they want in a conflict situation.

- ### *STEP 3: Pick a Plan—Stay and Make a Deal (Negotiate)*

   Students will learn the strategy of making a deal in a conflict situation.

Overview of the ASSIST Program

Affective/**S**ocial **S**kills: **I**nstructional **S**trategies and **T**echniques

The ASSIST Program is designed to increase students' growth in self-esteem, self-management, interpersonal relationships, conflict resolution, and emotional understanding. ASSIST manuals provide a complete guide for elementary school teachers and counselors to actively involve students in developing critical personal/social skills. The ASSIST Program can be used as a K-6 developmental school guidance curriculum by following the scope and sequence presented in Appendix B. It can be integrated into regular academic programs, or each manual can stand alone as a curriculum for personal growth or social competence.

The ASSIST curriculum is the result of an extensive review of child development theory and research, a review of existing social/emotional education programs, and the feedback of many teachers and students who participated in the program. ASSIST incorporates concepts and procedures from social learning theory, child psychology, and proven educational practices.

Each field-tested lesson includes:

- A "To the Teacher" section which provides a theoretical background for the lesson concepts;

- A "scripted" lesson that provides the dialogue, examples, and practice necessary to teach the lesson concepts and skills;

- A series of transparency masters which make the lesson concepts accessible to picture-smart students;

- A series of reproducible worksheets which provide opportunities for students to process the lessons; and

- A variety of "Supplementary Activities" designed to encourage the transfer of training.

ASSIST was developed with Title IV-C Innovative Education Funds and was evaluated in elementary school classrooms in four school districts. **Statistically significant gains in self-concept and social skills occurred in eight out of nine assessments.** As a result, ASSIST was validated in Washington State and designated cost-effective and exportable. It is now in the state's "Bank of Proven Practices," a clearinghouse for quality programs.

The ASSIST manuals currently in print include the following:

- ***Building Self-Esteem in the Classroom***—In both the *Primary Version* and the *Intermediate Version* students refine their self-descriptions and acquire an appreciation for their uniqueness. They learn that they are multifaceted and that there are at least seven different ways they can be smart. They learn the cognitive skill of self-encouragement, which enables them to respond to mistakes, failures, or put-downs in a manner which maintains their self-esteem. They learn to take responsibility for their school success by using self-statements to motivate and coach themselves through academic tasks. A unit written for advanced or middle school students is also included in the *Intermediate Version*. (*Primary Version*, 926 pages; *Intermediate Version*, 670 pages)

- ***Creating A Caring Classroom***—This manual includes a collection of strategies designed to promote mutual support and strengthen connections in the classroom. Included are (1) getting-acquainted activities; (2) classroom management procedures; (3) a personal/social behavior scale and behavior improvement strategies for students with special needs; (4) a relaxation training program; and (5) a large collection of activities for establishing a nurturing classroom community. (400 pages)

- ***Helping Kids Find Their Strengths***—This manual is designed to enable students to identify and utilize their strengths. It is based on the combined expertise of the theorists, researchers, and practitioners who worked on the Dependable Strengths Project Team at the University of Washington. Students are able to build their self-esteem not just by positive thinking but by analyzing experiences they're proud of for clues regarding their core strengths. Students share their good experiences, then utilize teacher and peer input to "tease out" the strengths that helped them create those experiences. They learn a large strength vocabulary and are able to prove to themselves and others that they have strengths they can depend on. They use their expanded self-identity as a springboard for new successes. In helping one another find their strengths, students develop a respect for diversity. (713 pages)

- ***Helping Kids Handle Anger***—This manual includes lessons designed to enable students to acknowledge, accept, and constructively express anger. Students learn: (1) to use inner speech to inhibit aggressive behaviors; (2) to use thinking skills for choosing constructive behaviors when angry; (3) appropriate language for expressing anger; (4) a variety of techniques for releasing energy after anger arousal; (5) ways to defuse the anger of others; and (6) a model for resolving classroom conflicts. Role-plays and puppets are utilized to encourage active student involvement. (516 pages)

- ***Helping Kids Handle Put-Downs***—This manual teaches students a repertoire of assertive responses to teasing that will not reinforce their antagonizers. Students learn the art of ignoring; how to surprise aggressors by "agreeing" with them; how to disarm aggressors with humor; and how to deflect aggression with "crazy compliments." These strategies win respect and de-escalate conflict. Students also learn to use self-encouragement to dispel the hurt of put-downs and maintain their self-respect. This volume contains both a *Primary Version* and *Intermediate Version*. (283 pages)

- ***Multiple Intelligences: Helping Kids Discover the Many Ways They're Smart***—The purpose of this manual is to help students understand that they are intellectually multifaceted. They are introduced to a process to assess their own strong intelligences. Students learn that each intelligence is as valuable as any other and gain respect for their own particular strengths, as well as those of others. The lessons in this manual are an expanded version of a unit on multiple intelligence in *Building Self-Esteem in the Classroom*. Additionally, this new manual contains a section of activities linking multiple intelligences with career choices. (333 pages)

- ***Teaching Cooperation Skills***—This manual includes a series of lessons and experiential activities designed to teach students the skills necessary for cooperative learning to take place. Lessons focus on the skills of self-management, listening, collaborative problem solving, and leadership. Students learn to resolve conflicts through negotiation and compromise. Included are 52 activities designed to provide practice of cooperation skills and 55 cooperative academic activities in the major subject areas. (437 pages)

- ***Teaching Friendship Skills***—Both the *Primary Version* and the *Intermediate Version* contain all new lessons and supplementary activities for each grade level. Students identify the behaviors in others which attract them and behaviors which alienate them. They examine their own behavior and determine changes they need to make in order to gain friends. They learn how to curb physical and verbal aggression. They discover that the secret to making friends is to make others feel special, and they practice specific ways to do so. They learn the value of sharing and how to give sincere compliments and apologies. In addition, the *Intermediate Version* focuses on listening, understanding others' perspectives and feelings, and being honest but kind. It also contains 56 activities designed for a "Friendship Center." Each version provides a comprehensive bibliography of children's books on friendship. Puppets, games, role-plays, kinesthetic activities, and goal-setting are used to increase motivation and the transfer of training. (*Primary Version*, 537 pages; *Intermediate Version*, 605 pages)

- ***Helping Kids Handle Conflict***—Through the lessons and activities presented in this manual, students learn to reduce verbal and physical violence through self-control, critical thinking, negotiation, and other strategies. These skills, applied through the Stop, Think, and Pick a Plan (STP) process, help students understand how to handle their own conflicts and when it is appropriate to seek adult assistance. Lessons 1 through 7 teach the STP process, from self-calming techniques, to deciding if it's best to walk away from a situation, to options available once the choice is made to either leave the disagreement or stay and try to work things out. Lesson 8 teaches students how to apply that process when dealing with bullies. (*Primary Version*, 460 pages)

Introduction

Schools are faced with a surprising number and variety of conflicts every day. Some of these conflicts involve overt behaviors such as yelling or pushing. Others are packaged in more subtle forms such as an irritating look or the quiet exclusion of someone from an activity.

Some conflicts involve big issues; some involve small issues. Competition, intolerance (cliques), opposing needs, inappropriate expressions of emotion, poor communication, and displays of power are just some of the issues that trigger conflicts between students. Conflicts arise over who sits by whom, who plays with whom or what, who is bugged by whom, who's better than whom, and the list goes on! Sometimes the conflicts end in laughter, sometimes in hurt feelings, sometimes in cuts and bruises.

Understanding Conflict

Whether in the classroom, on the playground, at home, or in the neighborhood, conflict is a normal part of life. When most people think of "conflict," they think of it in negative terms. Images such as destruction, war, battle, or fighting are evoked. These negative associations with the word come from experiences with unresolved conflicts. When conflicts go unmanaged or unresolved, they can have some pretty adverse outcomes!

Yet every conflict has within it the seeds for growth. While unmanaged conflict has negative, destructive results, conflict that is effectively managed can teach students about themselves and others. Research shows that improvement in students' ability to positively handle conflicts increases social support and decreases victimization, promotes mental health, facilitates positive attitudes toward life, and enhances self-esteem and internal locus of control. Conflicts can thus be a positive part of daily living and of the educational process.

Developing Skills for Resolving Conflicts

Many conflicts escalate or go unresolved because students do not have the necessary skills to handle them successfully. By learning and practicing positive approaches to conflict situations, students gain an increased understanding of themselves and others, learn to respect and accept differences, and learn self-control and the appropriate expression of emotions such as anger and frustration. As students learn conflict resolution skills, they become equipped to respond creatively to conflict situations rather than to respond with coercive, destructive behaviors.

Research shows that both bullies and their targets have a limited ability to solve conflicts. As bullies continue to pick on their targets and as the targets continue to find themselves bullied, they each develop patterns of response that eventually become part of their personality. It is important to teach children conflict resolution skills before these aggressive/passive behaviors become personality traits. By learning assertion, communication, and negotiation skills, students are preparing themselves for living in a diverse and multicultural world.

The purpose of the lessons in this manual is to reduce verbal and physical violence by teaching self-control, critical thinking, negotiation, and other conflict resolution strategies. The lessons aim at increasing student knowledge of nonviolent techniques for resolving conflicts and increasing students' ability to peacefully resolve conflict situations. The goal is that students will grow in their ability to handle their own conflicts and will learn when seeking adult assistance is and is not appropriate. To help students acquire the necessary knowledge and skills, the lessons teach a proven process for handling conflicts successfully. The process is called Stop, Think, and Pick a Plan, or STP.

Lesson 1 introduces students to the STP process and teaches them the important first step: Stop. Students learn and practice the self-calming techniques of "stopping" and "breathing" to de-escalate conflict situations.

Lesson 2 presents the "think" step. The lesson gives students practice in deciding whether it is smarter in a conflict situation to walk away or to stay.

In **Lessons 3-6** students learn the "pick a plan" step of STP. They are presented with eight different plans for handling conflict situations. Three of the plans come into play when students decide the smart thing to do is to leave a disagreement. Those plans are to get help, to go do something else, and to take time to cool down. The other five plans come into play when students decide that they will stay in the conflict situation and try to work things out. Those plans are to ignore the provocation, to tell the other person(s) what you want, to make a deal (negotiate), to use chance, and to say you're sorry.

Lesson 7 provides a review of the STP steps. Students are given a chance to demonstrate their understanding of the concepts and to apply the concepts to real-life situations.

Lesson 8 addresses the issue of bullying. Students learn how to handle bullying by applying some of the STP plans to various bullying situations.

There are four components involved in behavior change: a physiological component, a feeling component, a thinking component, and a doing component. Students have the most control over the doing component and some control over their thinking. They have little control over the feeling or physiological components. For this reason, the conflict resolution lessons in this manual focus on the thinking and doing aspects of student behavior. As students employ the STP process, the "thinking and doing" changes they make in handling their disagreements with others can begin to affect their thoughts and feelings as well.

Conflict Resolution: Life Skills

For the Stop, Think, and Pick a Plan (STP) process to have the greatest impact on reducing violent, coercive behaviors and increasing positive approaches to handling problems, it should be an integral part of life in your classroom and school. When the conflict resolution techniques presented in these lessons are implemented within the daily life of the classroom, learning is greatly increased. Real life is the best teacher of conflict resolution skills. When problems arise in the classroom, you as a teacher have an opportunity to walk students through the process of solving the conflicts themselves rather than solving the conflicts for them. Through these real-life situations, you can show them that often they can handle conflicts themselves rather than relying upon an adult to intervene.

It is also important that you as the teacher model the conflict resolution process and strategies being taught. Students will learn from the way in which you deal with conflict in everyday classroom and school situations. You need to "walk the talk," because teaching with actions is more powerful than teaching with just words. In addition to modeling the behaviors during the ordinary life experiences that are a part of your classroom, we recommend that you share your own life experiences, both good and bad choices, with your students so that they can learn from your successes and failures.

Beyond a classroom application of STP, a schoolwide implementation will further enhance the mastery and impact of STP. When a schoolwide program is implemented, the school becomes a productive environment in which the focus is on learning and having fun. For this reason, suggestions for schoolwide implementation and themes have been included in this manual. The skills students gain in these conflict resolution lessons are skills that they will be able to use not only at school but also at home and in their neighborhoods. They are skills they will use to handle conflict situations at home and on the job for the rest of their lives.

Important Resource

The lessons in this curriculum were created for use in the classroom, but they are also valuable as part of inservice training. For the latter purpose, it is recommended that they be used in conjunction with Randy Sprick's videotape inservice program entitled *STP Stop, Think, Plan: A School-Wide Conflict Resolution Strategy*. Like the ASSIST Program, Sprick's inservice program is available through Sopris West.

How to Use This Curriculum

Where to Use This Conflict Resolution Manual

The lessons in this manual can be used in several different arenas to teach conflict resolution skills to students. The classroom is a primary context for teaching these skills. They may be taught by a teacher or used by the school counselor as classroom guidance lessons. In addition, the lessons may be used in small counseling groups or when working with individual students. Lesson content and materials may also be used to promote a school-wide emphasis on conflict resolution. Additionally, they may be used by parents in the home and by teacher trainers during inservices on conflict resolution.

Lesson Grade Levels

This manual consists of lessons for primary students. Because of the timelessness and generality of the concepts found in these lessons, the same lessons can be taught to students as they advance through the primary grades. Each time students are exposed to the concepts in a given lesson, they are able to consider them from a new frame of reference and make new and more precise applications. Supplementary activities following each of the lessons can also be used at different grade levels to reinforce lesson concepts and assist students in applying what they have learned to daily life.

"To the Teacher" Section

Each lesson includes a clearly stated objective, a list of all the materials needed to teach the lesson, and a "To the Teacher" section. This section provides some theoretical background on the concepts presented. It also includes a summary of the skills to be taught in the lesson with suggestions for effective teaching.

"Lesson Presentation" Section

At the beginning of each lesson students are told specifically what they will learn in the lesson. Following the statement of the lesson objective, instructional input is given to students. Once the lesson concepts have been presented, the concepts are modeled through the use of positive examples and negative or non-examples. Students are then encouraged to practice the skills demonstrated in the positive examples through classroom discussion, role-plays, games, and discussion with learning partners. Learning partners are students sitting next to one another who are paired to discuss learning concepts under teacher direction. Each lesson ends with a summary, where lesson concepts are reviewed and homework is given to enhance the transfer of learning to daily life.

The "Lesson Presentation" section gives the teacher step-by-step instructions on how to conduct the lesson. To facilitate the use of teaching techniques, scripts are provided in bold-face type. These scripts are not intended to be used verbatim but instead are models of effective teacher comment and interaction. You will want to rephrase this script, saying things in your own words to accommodate aspects of your particular students' frames of reference. The puppet scripts and stories may be read verbatim, paraphrased, or even rewritten to incorporate examples, situations, and concerns most relevant to the lives of your particular students. The success of each lesson will depend on your ability to provide examples and illustrations of the lesson concepts that your students will readily relate to. It will also depend on your sense of how to pace the lesson, expanding or shortening sections to fit your students' needs.

Names of fictitious children are used throughout the lessons. It is important to substitute other names if there is any chance of embarrassment to your students. You may also wish to change names in order to focus positive attention on students of various ethnic origins.

Transparencies

Each lesson includes a series of transparency masters for picture-smart students whose learning style is "Don't just tell me—show me!" You may wish to color the transparencies or ask an "art-smart" student to do so. You'll be writing on some of the transparencies during the lesson and will need to clean the writing off afterward. Therefore, you'll need to use permanent-ink markers to color the transparencies. Berol Prismacolor™ Art Markers, which come in a wide variety of colors, are a good choice. If you color the transparencies on the back side, the markers will not dissolve the black lines of the transparencies.

Supplementary Activities

Following each lesson are a number of activities designed to appeal to students of varying abilities and interests. These activities are intended to help students process the ideas presented in the lesson and to provide opportunities for students to practice targeted conflict resolution skills. Many of these activities provide practice of basic academic skills as well.

Often, teachers have students complete these activities as part of the lesson. Another approach is to make an "STP" booklet for each student containing supplementary activity sheets from each lesson and have the students work on their booklets after you've taught the main lessons. This practice will keep the STP concepts fresh in the students' minds. You can provide added encouragement to the students by having the puppet Scruffy, used throughout the lessons, look at their booklets from time to time. You might ask the students to pick a page in their booklet that they would like Scruffy to see. Then you could have

Scruffy go around the classroom and look at the pages the students have chosen, making positive comments about their work.

Handouts/Homework

Reproducible student handouts/worksheets accompany each lesson and are given as homework for the students. These worksheets give students an opportunity to process lesson concepts presented during the week as well as to demonstrate that they were "attending and receiving" during the lesson presentation and discussion.

Posters

Each of the lessons has a poster or posters that can be used to remind students of key lesson concepts. After teaching each lesson be sure to display the poster(s) in a prominent place. When incidents of conflict occur in the classroom, refer to the poster(s) as you assist students in using the STP process, emphasizing the concepts they have just learned. In addition, a brightly colored 18" x 24" poster of the "Stop, Think, Pick a Plan" wheel is available from Sopris West for $6.00. It can be ordered by calling 1-800-547-6747. This colorful and catchy visual teaching tool provides students with a distillation of all of the lesson concepts presented in the curriculum and is a great prompt.

Scheduling the Lessons

Lessons should last 20-30 minutes for younger primary students and 30-45 minutes for older primary students, depending on the students' attention spans. Some lessons can be divided and taught in segments without lessening their effectiveness. Teaching the lesson early in the school day allows you to capitalize on opportunities during the remainder of the day to use the lesson vocabulary and encourage the students to use the skills that were introduced that morning.

Some teachers integrate these lessons into health, social studies, or language arts/communication curricula. Others set up a formal "personal/social skills" classroom time, teaching lessons once or twice per week during that time or using a "unit" format, in which they teach a lesson or conduct an activity on a daily basis for a period of time.

Lesson Preparation

When teaching a lesson, teachers need to be flexible enough to tailor it to the specific needs of their students. Doing so, however, requires that they be very familiar with the lesson before they teach it. The following are a few suggestions for gaining that familiarity:

- Tape a lesson and listen to it as you travel to and from school. The more familiar you become with the lesson format the freer you will be to "ad lib" the lesson during class and the more easily you will be able to handle the many transparencies that accompany the lesson.

- Read over the lesson and then go back and highlight the main points you want to use when teaching your class. The highlighted script can then be used as a jumping-off place for your own "ad libbing" of the lesson.

- You can copy the dialogue sections and use them verbatim at the proper time in the lesson. You may also wish to make notes about the lesson content on index cards for reference as you teach from the lesson transparencies.

Using Teachable Moments

Be alert for teachable moments—times at which you can verbally link present events to conflict resolution skills you have presented previously. Just as a single vitamin tablet administered on a regular basis is a more effective regimen than a handful once per month, growth in conflict resolution skills is more likely to occur with regular skill applications.

Here are several strategies you can use to create and enhance teachable moments:

- Pinpoint the STP skill or skills your students need practice with. For example, if a number of your students are having difficulty with tattling, focus on helping students take responsibility for handling their own conflict situations. Prompt students by asking them what they can do to solve the problem. Praise students when you see them working out a problem without your assistance. Noticing and commending students for using STP skills is a very powerful teaching tool.

- Capture student attention by calling "Freeze!" when you observe student interactions exemplifying STP behaviors that you want to reinforce. Immediately "debrief" the situation by wondering out loud, "This situation could have really caused a big argument between the two of you. What did you just do that stopped a little disagreement from turning into a big fight?" Praise the participants for working out their conflict peaceably.

- Slow down your rate of speech and use pauses when you are reinforcing an STP concept. By speaking more slowly you will increase the intensity and impact of what you are communicating. By pausing you will allow time for the students to process the information and respond.

- Use students' names and gain their attention before reinforcing a concept or giving a prompt to assist them in areas in which their conflict resolution skills are weak.

- Praise students when they demonstrate conflict resolution skills that they find difficult. For example, a student who has trouble with sharing or taking turns should be praised when he or she demonstrates that behavior in a conflict situation.

- Reinforce peer modeling by observing and commenting on students' use of STP skills. Give specific feedback by saying, for example, "I noticed that you both wanted to be first in line but John suggested taking turns. By making a deal with Paul, John helped stop a little argument from turning into a big fight."

- Use the same vocabulary with students, teachers, and parents when reinforcing and prompting the use of STP conflict resolution skills. A common vocabulary links the STP lesson concepts to the situations students face daily.

Integrating Lesson Concepts Into the Classroom

You can achieve maximum results with this curriculum by finding ways for students to practice and review the concepts regularly and by consistently extending the learning to other areas throughout the school year. Here are some suggestions for accomplishing this:

- Weave lesson concepts and activities into your art and creative writing programs.

- Use children's literature and movies to introduce a conflict resolution concept or to reinforce and extend concepts taught in the lessons. Examine characters' conflicts with one another and how they chose to resolve the conflicts. Encourage students to explain how the characters might have better solved the conflicts through use of the STP steps.

- Periodically repeat some of the games included in the lessons.

- Ask students to draw and/or share a specific time when they will implement a behavior encouraged in a lesson. Follow up by asking students to share their experiences with using the conflict resolution skill(s).

- Encourage students to do the assigned homework and spend a portion of subsequent lesson time reviewing the previous lesson's homework assignment.

- Display conflict resolution posters in the classroom so that students are reminded of the skills taught. Use the posters as a prompt for students when they need encouragement and guidance in learning to handle disputes without adult intervention.

- Start an STP Club for students who have consistently demonstrated the use of conflict resolution skills and have not been involved in negative responses to conflict during the day or week. Reward for membership could include a fun activity, an extra recess, or a special sticker.

- Use other suggestions found in the section on schoolwide implementation in this manual to further enhance student learning.

Suggestions for Enhancing the Teaching of This Curriculum

- As mentioned earlier, assign learning partners, pairs of students who can discuss lesson concepts when you direct them to do so.

- Write students' names on Popsicle sticks. Then, after asking students a question, draw a stick to determine who will be called on for a response. Drawing names in this way will assure randomness and will encourage all students to think of the answers to your questions, because they will not know who will be called on.

- Have students give "thumbs up" or "thumbs down" in response to general questions.

- Pique student interest in the lessons by using puppets to introduce the concepts and help students practice skills.

- Emphasize the fun activities that are a part of, or supplement to, each lesson.

- Make sure students keep all handouts and materials from the lessons in a special folder.

- Encourage student participation through classroom discussion and role-plays. Rather than trying to complete the lessons in a given time, let students' interests, responses, needs, and contributions shape the lessons.

- Incorporate supplementary activities into your language arts or art program.

Parent Involvement

Send home a parent letter, like that on page 15, before you begin teaching the conflict resolution lessons to inform parents of the curriculum and ask for their support. In addition, use the parent communication form "Keeping in Touch," which is printed on page 17, to inform parents of lesson activities as you proceed through the unit. Family members can then assist you by reinforcing the lesson concepts at home and helping the students to use the skills they have learned. After Lesson 7, send home the student letter that appears on page 18. Help students fill in the appropriate name of the adult they are going to give it to.

Letter to Family Member

Date _____

Dear Family Member,

I am writing to ask your support as we begin a unit in our classroom on handling and resolving conflicts. The skills we will be studying will be helpful to your child as he or she faces the inevitable conflict situations that are a part of everyday life.

Much of what our children learn from both television and the society in which we live promotes unhealthy or destructive responses to conflict. Our goal for this unit is to increase your child's repertoire of peacemaking skills so that he or she can respond creatively, constructively, and nonviolently to conflict. We want students to be able to think of a number of respectful and assertive responses to use (1) when they don't get what they want; (2) when someone insults them or hurts them; or (3) when someone treats them unfairly. By teaching children some universal and proven strategies, we hope to empower them to handle conflicts in ways that you and they will be proud of.

Here are some specific things that your child will be learning in this unit. We will be using the <u>S</u>top, <u>T</u>hink, and Pick a <u>P</u>lan approach, or STP. This approach emphasizes that it is important to stop a conflict before it escalates into violence. Kids are taught ways to stop and calm down in order to be able to **think** about the smart thing to do in the situation ("Should I walk away or should I stay?").

Without stopping and cooling down in conflict situations kids, and even adults, often make poor choices. Once kids are calm enough to think, they are ready to pick a **plan** of action. Plans that we will work on in the classroom are to get help, to walk away and do something else, to take more time to cool down, to ignore the provocation, to tell the other kid(s) what you want, to make a deal, to use chance, and to say you're sorry. (See the illustration attached to this letter.)

As parents and educators, we need to work together to help children learn strategies that can keep conflicts from escalating, damaging their self-esteem, and ruining their friendships. At home and school, we can work together to provide modeling, practice, and encouragement of self-management skills.

The following are some suggestions that you may find useful:

- Accept that arguments and fights between children are normal and view them as a part of your child's growing-up experience.

- Ask your child about the lessons on conflict management being taught at school.

- Remind your child to use the skills he or she has learned when your child is facing a conflict. Don't jump in and try to solve the conflict for your child.

- Use conflict situations in your home as opportunities to guide children through the "slow down and think of a plan" process.

- Give examples to your child of how you deal with conflicts with others at home, at work, and with friends.

- If you have an opportunity to model an appropriate way to deal with a conflict, ask your child what he or she saw or heard you say or do.

- Talk with your child about conflict situations viewed in movies or on television and discuss how the conflicts could have been resolved without violence, aggression, or unkindness.

By joining forces, we can work to stem the tide of violence in our society. The conflict resolution skills that will be taught in this unit will provide children with a foundation for getting along with others throughout their lives.

Sincerely,

STOP, THINK, AND PICK A PLAN

Keeping in Touch

Date _____

Dear Family Member,

- In our classroom your child is learning:

- Your child's homework this week is:

- If you wish, you can help by:

- If you have any questions or concerns, please call me at:

Thank you for your support.

Sincerely,

Student Letter to Family

Date _____

Dear _____,

In school I've been learning to use the <u>S</u>top, <u>T</u>hink, and Pick a <u>P</u>lan (STP) approach when I'm mad or when someone is bugging me. Now I'm trying to remember to use STP outside of school. Please listen to me explain how STP works and remind me if I forget to use it.

Thank you,

P.S. If I do a good job, will you please sign below?

_____

Lesson 1

Stop, Think, and Pick a Plan— A Conflict Resolution Process

STEP 1: Stop

Stop, Think, and Pick a Plan— A Conflict Resolution Process

STEP 1: Stop

Objective   Students will learn to identify the cues in themselves and in others that signal an escalating conflict.

Students will be introduced to a process they can use to de-escalate conflict.

Students will learn and practice the self-calming techniques of "stopping" and "breathing" to de-escalate conflicts.

Materials   Transparency #1 – "How Small Arguments Turn Into Big Fights"

Transparency #2/Handout #1 – "STP Traffic Light"

Transparency #3/Poster – "The Stop Step"

Handout #2 – "I Can STOP and Cool Down"

Puppet Masters #1A and #1B – "Scruffy the STP Dog" (make the puppet in advance or use a different puppet of your choice)

Red, yellow, and green transparency markers

To the Teacher

Conflict is a natural part of school life and life in general! Disagreements are inevitable because no two people have exactly the same wants. In the elementary school environment, as in all other school environments, fear and power struggles are present and can create significant disruptions to classroom learning. Even when a lot of effort is made to keep all students safe from put-downs, bullying, and conflicts, these behaviors are, at times, part of every student's life experience. For this reason, students need to become independent problem solvers and need to be given the skills to handle the inevitable quarrels that arise. When students are so equipped, teachers and students alike will have more time and energy to devote to academic tasks.

Conflict situations can be a positive growing experience or a destructive one for students. How students handle disagreements will determine whether the situation will be hurtful or growth enhancing. Disagreements can give students an opportunity to learn respect and appreciation of differences, to grow in their ability to see another's point of view, and to develop negotiation skills. For many students, knowledge of how to handle conflicts and disagreements is acquired haphazardly, often from TV or movies that emphasize aggressive methods. Students need to have systematic teaching of how to stop disagreements from escalating and how to resolve them in a calm, controlled, and peaceful manner. They need to acquire a repertoire of ways to appropriately respond to interpersonal conflict.

This lesson introduces students to a simple process they can employ for working through conflicts without aggression or coercion. The approach is called STP: Stop, Think, and Pick a Plan. It emphasizes slowing down one's behavior and taking the time to think when conflict occurs. It is modeled on the notion of a traffic signal. The red light represents stopping or calming down, the amber light represents thinking of the "smart" thing to do (walk away from the conflict situation or stay and work it out), and the green light represents planning a way to handle the conflict and going forward with that plan. Through practice in this process, students learn increased self-control and reflective thinking skills.

This lesson focuses on stopping and calming down. The benefits of a calming-down technique are that it prevents the buildup of intense feelings and allows students to think of productive ways to handle anger-provoking incidents. Students will be shown how to tell when small problems are heading toward big fights by noticing cues in themselves and in others. By observing such cues as clenched fists, louder voice volume, name-calling, and a red or hot face, students can identify the escalation of a conflict and decide to employ the first step in the STP process: Stop.

The "stop" step is a key component in the process. Students will not find it naturally easy to stop themselves as a conflict is escalating. So it is important for them to learn techniques for stopping and calming down. Two particularly effective techniques are taught in this lesson. One is to say or think "Stop!" while visualizing a big stop sign. By giving themselves the "stop" command, students will automatically slow themselves (and the escalating tension of the disagreement) down. For some situations and/or personalities this technique will be sufficient. But when it is not, a second technique that can be used is to take in more oxygen. This relaxes the body muscles, reversing the escalation of tension.

Because the "stop" step is so critical to the process of positive conflict resolution and because it is not a natural tendency, students will need a lot of practice using this technique if they are to generalize it to the real-life situations they encounter in the classroom, at recess, and in their other interpersonal encounters. The role-plays in this lesson will help students see how the techniques they are being taught can become a part of how they normally approach conflict situations. The strategy of the lesson is to tell students what to do, show them how to do it, and provide them with multiple practice opportunities that will reinforce their learning. In addition, a handout activity is provided that can be completed in class or given as homework. This simple activity, in which students identify their body signs signaling when it is time to stop and calm down, provides another opportunity for the transfer of learning from the formal teaching setting into daily student discourse.

A key factor in assisting students to become successful at resolving conflict is to incorporate the strategies students are being taught into the day-to-day activities of the classroom. At the end of this lesson, we recommend that you display the poster "The Stop Step," which reinforces the lesson concepts, in a place where students will be able to use it as a reminder for the rest of the week. At times during the school day model the calming down steps. Look for occasions during the day when it would be appropriate for you to employ the calming down steps. Also look for times when it would be appropriate for students to use the calming-down techniques learned in this lesson and prompt them to do so.

Lesson Presentation

IT'S NORMAL TO HAVE DISAGREEMENTS

We're going to be spending some time taking a look at conflicts, such as arguments and fights. By the end of this lesson you will be better at noticing when a small problem is starting to turn into a serious fight or argument. You will also learn some steps you can use to slow down a fight so that you can take control and avoid a bunch of trouble when you get into conflicts with others.

Have any of you ever argued or had a conflict with other kids about what you wanted to do during recess? Raise your thumb if you have.

How many of you have ever had an argument about who should go first when you're doing something together? *Have students respond to this and the remaining questions with the "thumbs up or down" technique.*

Have any of you ever had a disagreement with someone about following the rules of a game?

Have any of you ever gotten really mad because someone was bugging you?

Is there anyone in here who has ever gotten into a disagreement with a good friend? It looks like just about everyone in here has disagreements or conflicts now and then. That includes me, so I guess you could say that having conflicts in our lives is one thing we all have in common.

Is it normal for people to get mad at each other once in a while? As a matter of fact, it's just about impossible to not have conflicts with others because we each have our own ideas and feelings about things. No two people think or feel the same way about everything. Even good friends argue or have disagreements.

What are some typical disagreements or conflicts that kids your age tend to have? *Record responses on a blank transparency or chalkboard so they can be used as role-play ideas later.*

SMALL DISAGREEMENTS CAN ESCALATE INTO CONFLICTS

Puppet

We've just listed some perfectly normal everyday disagreements and examples of times when normal disagreements can grow into big fights. Did you know that you have within yourself the ability to stop disagreements from turning into fights? The first step is to recognize when a disagreement is starting to turn into a fight, because it's at that point that it's easiest to slow things down and not say or do things you'll regret later. I think I can show you what I'm talking about by doing a role-play with a friend of mine. *Conduct the role-play with the "Scruffy" puppet, making actions appropriate to the role-play.*

Teacher: **This is my friend Scruff. He doesn't know what the letters "STP" on his shirt stand for, but by the end of this lesson we'll all know.** (To Scruff) **Say "Hi" to the class, Scruff.**

Scruff: **Hi, guys!**

Teacher: **How have things been going for you lately, Scruff?**

Scruff: *(In a discouraged voice)* **O.K., I guess.**

Teacher: **Sounds like you're feeling kind of low.**

Scruff: **Yeah, well. My friend and I are mad at each other. I don't know why, but we always get into these big fights over nothing.**

Teacher: **Oh, we were just talking about something like that. Does it start out as a disagreement and then grow into a big fight?**

Scruff: **Yeah. Like yesterday at recess. I wanted to play Four Square and my friend wanted to play soccer. We ended up in a big fight!**

Teacher: **Gee, Scruff, I can see why you seem down. Why don't we role-play the situation and see if the class can help figure out what happened. You be you and I'll pretend to be your friend. O.K.?**

Scruff: **O.K.**

Teacher: **Class, you can help Scruff by watching this role-play and looking for the point at which the normal disagreement Scruff and I are we're having starts turning into a big problem or conflict. Scruff, let's get started.**

Scruff: **Hey, let's play Four Square this recess.**

Teacher: **I thought we were going to play soccer this recess.**

Scruff: **Four Square would be more fun. We always play soccer.**

Teacher: **No we don't. I don't want to play Four Square.**

Scruff: *(Starts to raise voice and get mad)* **We always do what you want. I'm sick of soccer.**

Teacher: *(In a loud voice)* **Why are you getting so mad? I think soccer's fun.**

Scruff: *(Using rude tone of voice and animated body language)* **I'm not mad—I just think soccer is boring! I'll find somebody else to play with.**

Teacher: **Oh, come on. Don't be so bossy!**

Scruff: **You're the one who's bossy. Get out of my way, Jerk. I'm going.** *(Starts to push teacher out of the way.)*

Teacher: **Fine! See if I ever play with you again.** *(Stomps off.)*

O.K., class. I'm going to let Scruff sit over here while we discuss the role-play. *(Pick a place to put Scruff while you discuss the role-play with the class.)* **I'm sure you noticed that the disagreement started out with Scruff wanting to do one thing and me wanting to do something else. For friends, this is a perfectly normal type of disagreement. But there was a point at which things started turning into a big argument.**

Write students' responses to the following questions on the overhead or chalkboard.

What are some things you saw or heard that told you we were getting angrier?

What did we do with our voices?

What did we do with our bodies?

Good noticing! It's important to realize when a small argument is starting to turn into a big conflict.

Transp. #1

Show Transparency #1, "How Small Arguments Turn Into Big Fights." Summarize the comments just made by saying: **It's things like** *(point as you read)* **talking really loudly or in a mean, snotty tone of voice, name-calling, yelling, pushing, and hitting that cause an everyday, normal disagreement to get out of control.**

In the role-play, if Scruff or I had noticed right about here *(on Transparency #1 draw a vertical line right before "mean tone of voice")* **that our tones of voice were changing and that we were talking louder and meaner, we could have done something to slow things**

down . . . and we wouldn't have ended up being so mad at each other.

Why would you want to keep disagreements from turning into big, angry fights? *Solicit responses from students, pointing out that fighting is against school rules, can ruin friendships, and will just bring trouble.*

INTRODUCING STP

I want to show you a trick both Scruff and you can use right at this point *(point to the vertical line you drew on the transparency)* **so you don't end up getting into a big fight over something really picky.**

| Transp. #2 | *Put Transparency #2, "STP Traffic Light," on the overhead. It is suggested here that you color the lights as you explain what each represents. Just as effective is to color the lights ahead of time and slide a piece of paper down the transparency to uncover the lights one at a time as you talk about them.* **As you can see, this is a traffic light with the words "Stop," "Think," and "Pick a Plan" written on the lights. It illustrates a trick people can use to stay out of trouble. We call it STP for short. It's written on Scruff's shirt. What does STP stand for?** |

Thinking of a traffic light helps when you're in a conflict because the first thing you need to remember to do is to stop. *Color the stop circle red on the transparency.* **It's kind of like putting on the brakes. This is one of the most important things to do when you're in a conflict. Stopping for a second can keep you from saying something stupid or getting yourself in trouble. Stopping gives you a chance to think.**

Color the think circle yellow.

One of the reasons conflicts develop into big fights is because people forget to stop and think. The yellow light gives you some time to do this. It gives you time to shift gears. Instead of racing into a big fight, you slow down and use your brain. You ask yourself, "What's the smart thing to do here? Should I walk away or stay?"

After you've let yourself know that you <u>can</u> control yourself and after you've decided whether the best thing for you to do is walk away from the situation or stay in it, you're ready for the green light.

Color the pick a plan circle green.

You're ready to pick a plan that will make the situation better. Your choices are (1) to stay and talk with the person you're having

a conflict with or ignore what they are doing OR (2) to walk away so the situation doesn't get worse. You're ready to plan a smart solution and go with it.

By using these three simple steps—<u>S</u>top, <u>T</u>hink, and Pick a <u>P</u>lan—you can take control of any conflict situation you run into. We'll call these steps STP.

| Transp. #1 | *Show Transparency #1 again.* **The most important thing to keep in mind is that when you realize a conflict is starting with someone, you need to slow things down. You need to stop and think. That's a way to guarantee that the types of behaviors shown on this transparency won't happen and that you won't end up in trouble.** *Point to each of the behaviors on the transparency.* **That's the only way you'll be able to come up with a solution that is smart and keep small arguments from turning into big fights.**

SAY OR THINK "STOP!"

People have different techniques they use to get themselves to stop and think. Some people count to ten to help themselves cool down. Do any of you do that? Some people even count to ten backwards. These are good methods. I'd like to show you another one that also works really well.

| Transp. #3 | *Show Transparency #3, "The <u>S</u>top Step," covering the bottom line of type.* **With this method of cooling down you think of a big red stop sign and you say the word "Stop!" to yourself. Here's an example. Imagine that somebody took the ball at recess when it was your turn to use it and you're so mad you feel like hitting the kid who took it. Now, I want you to close your eyes and imagine a big red stop sign with the word "STOP" on it. Raise your thumb if you're picturing it. Now, say "Stop!" out loud.** *After students do this, say:* **Now, say "Stop!" to yourself.** *Pause.* **How many of you think you would be less likely to lose your temper if you said "Stop!" to yourself?**

TAKING DEEP BREATHS

For some people this method is enough to keep them from losing their temper. Other people need to do more—they need to take **some deep breaths.** *Uncover "Take a deep breath and blow out your anger" on the transparency.* **Getting a lot of air into your body when you are starting to lose your temper is the <u>best</u> way to cool yourself down** and keep yourself out of trouble. When we're mad, our bodies get tense to prepare us to fight back or run away. Our chests tighten up, and we take smaller breaths. When we're all tensed up, it's hard to think, and when we don't think, we often do dumb things. We need to calm our bodies down when we're angry so we can think about the best thing to do. The quickest way to do that is by taking some deep breaths.

Let's say that I feel really angry with all of you because when you came in from recess I asked you three or four times to calm down and get in your seats but you're still not quiet. I'm so mad, I need to calm down so that I can think about the lesson I am going to teach you. The first thing I'm going to do is imagine a red stop sign and say "Stop!" to myself. *Model this.* Now, I'm going to take a deep breath to help calm myself down some more. *Model this.* Whew, I feel a little better. It's kind of like I blew some of my anger out when I breathed the air out!

I want you to imagine again that somebody took the ball at recess when it was your turn to use it. You're so mad you feel like hitting the kid who took it. Now imagine that big red stop sign and say "Stop!" to yourself. Now take a big deep breath. Now take another deep breath, and this time let your anger blow out with the air. Notice how your body feels after you let the air out. Does anybody want to describe how they felt when they did that?

PRACTICING THE STOP AND BREATHE TECHNIQUES

Now that you know what to do to keep yourself cool during an argument, I'd like you to use what you learned to help Scruff and me. We'll do the role-play again that we did earlier. This time, I want you to you call out "Stop!" when you think we need to start cooling down. *Do the same role-play with Scruff that you did at the beginning of the lesson. When students call out "Stop!" have Scruff model saying "Stop!" to himself and taking a deep breath.*

Let's practice calming down a few more times. Who can tell me some times when kids your age need to work hard to control their temper? *List examples on the board or overhead and use the best ones to provide further practice for students in utilizing the stop and breathe process. Invite students to model these skills. Have them say "Stop!" out loud, explaining that they would say it to themselves in a real conflict.*

HOMEWORK AND LESSON SUMMARY

Give students a large piece of construction paper. Ask them to fold it in half, like a book cover, and write the letters STP on the front in red, yellow, and green, respectively. Explain that they can use this as a folder to hold the handouts they will be getting during the next few lessons.

Handout #1
Handout #2

Give students Handout #1, "STP Traffic Light." Tell them that for home-work they should color the three traffic lights, being careful that the words still show. Also give students Handout #2, "I Can STOP and Cool Down," to complete as a homework assignment.

Then say: **Let's review what we talked about in this lesson. When you get into an argument or conflict, how can you stop yourself from getting really angry and saying something you might regret?** *Allow for student response. Then summarize:* **Good! A helpful tech-nique is to think of a big red stop sign, say or think "Stop!" and take a deep breath, breathing out your anger.**

Over the next few days I want you to be on the alert for times when someone is in an argument and needs to stop and calm themselves down. You might also look for examples of this when you are watching TV. Keep an eye on yourself, too. See if you can figure out when you're starting to get really mad and need to use the "stop and calm down" step. If you happen to get into an argument with someone, try to use this technique to stop yourself so you don't do or say anything you'll be sorry for later. In our next lesson you'll learn another clever technique to help you stay in control when you're mad.

Summarize the lesson by having students complete one or more of the fol-lowing sentence stems:

- **I learned ...**

- **STP could be helpful when ...**

- **What I'd like to know is ...**

- **Something in this lesson I might use is ...**

SUPPLEMENTARY ACTIVITIES

Use the supplementary activities that follow this lesson to reinforce the lesson concepts.

- *Signs My Body Gives Me Telling Me That It's Time to Stop and Calm Down*
  (Supplementary Activity #1)

- *How I Usually Act When Someone Is Bugging Me*
  (Supplementary Activity #2)

- *Things I Can Say to Myself to Cool Down When I'm Angry*
  (Supplementary Activity #3)

- *The Face of ANGER*
  (Supplementary Activity #4)

TRANSPARENCY #1

How Small Arguments Turn Into Big Fights

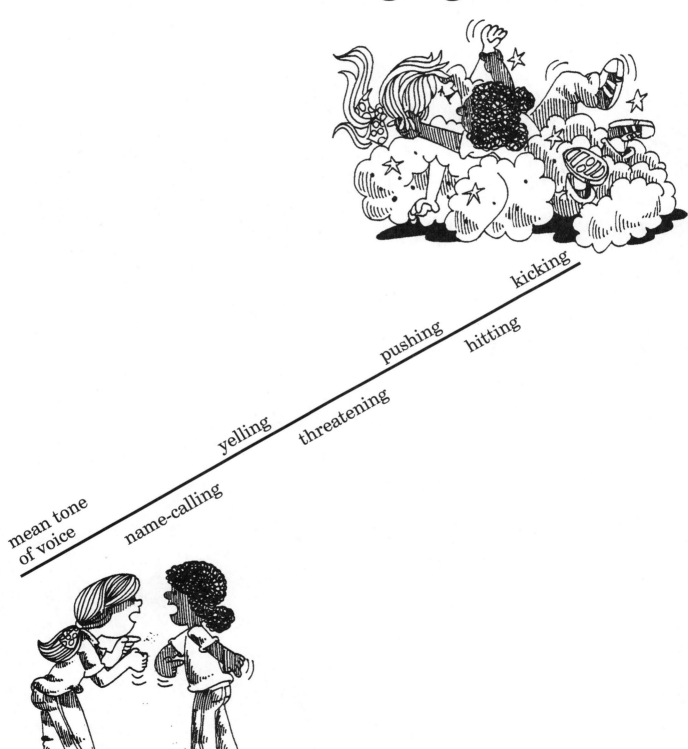

TRANSPARENCY #2/HANDOUT #1

STP Traffic Light

TRANSPARENCY #3/POSTER

The <u>S</u>top Step

- **Think or say "STOP!"**

- **Take a deep breath and blow out your anger.**

HANDOUT #2

I Can STOP and Cool Down

Fill in the blanks below with two things you should do during the STOP step.

• **Think or say __ __ __ __!**

• **Take a deep breath and blow __ __ __ your anger.**

PUPPET MASTER #1A

Scruffy the STP Dog

Glue head to bottom of paper bag.

Glue body (on Puppet Master #1B page) to side of paper bag.

PUPPET MASTER #1B

Scruffy the STP Dog

SUPPLEMENTARY ACTIVITY #1

Signs My Body Gives Me Telling Me That It's Time to Stop and Calm Down

1. Underline the sentences below which describe what happens to you when you start to get angry.
2. Draw a line from those sentences to the part of the outlined figure that represents where the body sign occurs in your body.
3. Draw yourself in the outline.

My hands feel like pushing or hitting.

I start talking louder.

I talk with a mean voice.

My stomach feels weird.

My heart beats faster.

I clench my teeth.

My hands feel like throwing things.

My brain starts thinking of all kinds of mean things to say.

I start to feel hot.

My feet feel like kicking.

SUPPLEMENTARY ACTIVITY #2

How I Usually Act When Someone Is Bugging Me

Put a check (✓) in front of the sentences that tell some of the ways you typically act when another kid bugs you.

- ❏ Ignore it
- ❏ Get help from a grown-up
- ❏ Talk about it with the other kid
- ❏ Make the other kid apologize
- ❏ Yell
- ❏ Hit, push, or kick someone

- ❏ Feel afraid to say how you feel
- ❏ Get friends to gang up on the other kid
- ❏ Clench your hands
- ❏ Call the kid a name
- ❏ Count to ten
- ❏ Tattle on the person

- ❏ Blow up
- ❏ Walk away or leave the situation
- ❏ Tear up a paper or an old magazine
- ❏ Take deep breaths to calm down
- ❏ Throw something
- ❏ Leave and say mean things about the person to others

How many sentences did you check? _____

How many of the things you checked are good ways to handle being bugged? _____

Circle all the positive ways listed on this page for handling being bugged.

SUPPLEMENTARY ACTIVITY #3

Things I Can Say to Myself to Cool Down When I'm Angry

Below are examples of calming things to say to yourself to help you cool down when you're angry. Circle the two that you like the best.

1. "I won't make a big deal about it."

2. "It's not worth it to get angry."

3. "I'm not going to let this get to me."

4. "I won't get into a fight over this."

5. "I won't be a fool—I'll keep my cool."

6. "As long as I keep cool, I'm in control."

7. "She (he) would like to make me mad. Well, I'm going to disappoint her (him)."

8. "I won't be mean."

9. "I'm not going to get myself in trouble."

Write your favorite one here:

_____

_____

_____

SUPPLEMENTARY ACTIVITY #4

The Face of *ANGER*

Cut out and arrange the puzzle pieces from the handout to create an angry face in the outline below. Then read the words on the puzzle to learn behaviors that make arguments worse.

SUPPLEMENTARY ACTIVITY #4 HANDOUT

The Face of *ANGER*

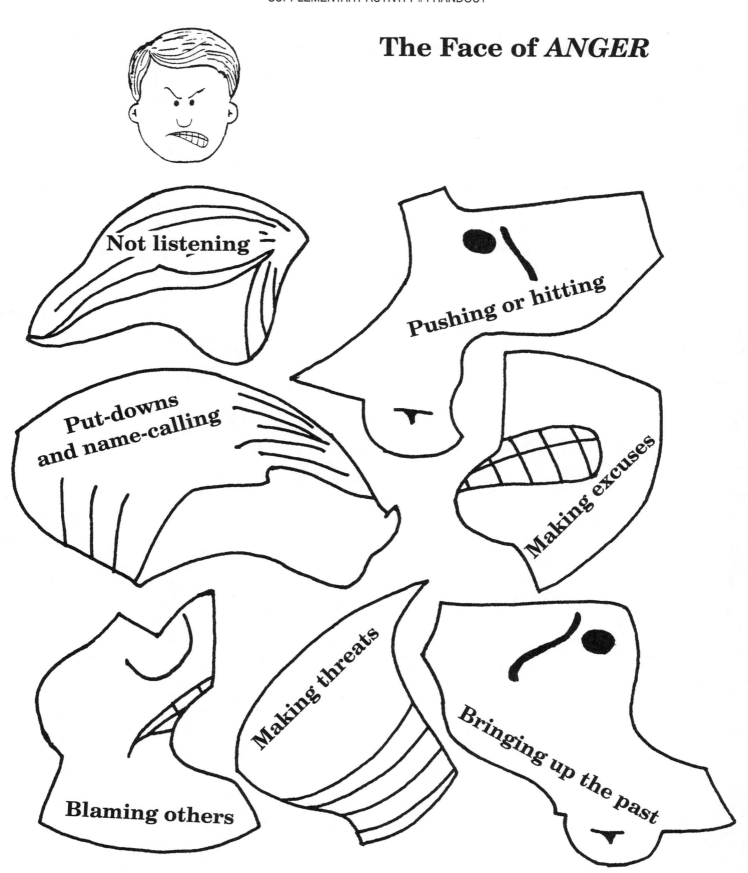

Lesson 2

Stop, Think, and Pick a Plan—
A Conflict Resolution Process

STEP 2: Think

Stop, Think, and Pick a Plan— A Conflict Resolution Process

STEP 2: Think

Objective   Students will practice determining whether they should walk away or stay in a conflict situation.

Materials   Transparency #2 from Lesson 1 – "STP Traffic Light"

Transparency #1/Handout #1/Poster – "The Think Step"

Transparency #2 – "The Big Question: Walk Away or Stay?"

Transparency #3/Handout #2 – "I Can Stop and THINK"

One piece of blank paper for each student

Scruffy the STP Dog puppet from Lesson 1

To the Teacher

In this lesson students are introduced to the "think" step of the STP process. They will learn to ask themselves the key question when faced with a conflict: "What is the smart thing to do: walk away or stay?" The goal is for students to learn to utilize the time gained by inhibiting their impulses, the skill they practiced in Lesson 1, to think about the best thing to do next. By framing this process as an "intelligent" behavior, teachers can encourage students to respect themselves for choosing nonviolent solutions to disagreements. By thinking rather than reacting emotionally, students can begin the process of resolving conflicts peacefully.

When teaching students to ask themselves if they should walk away or stay in a conflict situation, it is important to emphasize that either decision can be an intelligent choice. Students will learn to ask themselves, "Will I get hurt?" and "Will I get myself in trouble?" to help them in this key decision-making step.

Students need a great deal of practice with this "think" step. By mastering this cognitive process, they will have laid the foundation for going on to the next step, utilizing specific conflict resolution strategies, or "picking a plan." To help make the "stop" and "think" steps a norm in the classroom, students are asked to remind one another in a friendly way to use these two steps during the week. At the end of this lesson, we recommend that you display the poster entitled, "The Think Step," which reinforces the lesson concept, in a place where students will be able to use it as a reminder for the rest of the week.

Lesson Presentation

LESSON 1 REVIEW: THE "STOP" STEP

Lesson 1, Transp. #2

Last time we learned how little disagreements can turn into big arguments or fights. We also learned about the STP steps for handling fights or conflict. Raise your thumb if you remember what the "S" stands for in STP. When I count to three, shout out the word. *Count to three and allow students to shout "Stop!"* **That's right: Stop!** *Show Transparency #2 from Lesson 1, "STP Traffic Light," and point to the red circle.* **When you start to get mad, there are three things you can do at the "stop" step to cool off. Who can tell me one?** *Allow for student responses.* **That's right. You can imagine a big red stop sign, you can say or think "Stop!" and you can take a deep breath and blow out your anger.** *Model and then have students go through the three parts of the STOP step themselves.*

Puppet

Put the Scruffy puppet on your hand. Say: **Do you remember Scruff from the last lesson? Let's see how well Scruff did in the past week in cooling himself down when he found himself having a disagreement with a friend.**

Teacher: **Hi, Scruff! Would you like to say "Hi" to the class?**

Scruff: **Hi, guys.**

Teacher: *(After class greets Scruff)* **Scruff, we've just been remembering the three things we can do to stop ourselves from turning a little disagreement into a big argument. Did you run into any disagreements with any of your friends this week in which you tried to stop yourself from making things worse?**

Scruff: **Yeah. My friend Monty and I started arguing about which Nintendo game to play. I felt myself getting <u>mad</u>!**

Teacher: **So what did you do?**

Scruff: **I was just getting ready to growl really loudly at Monty when I remembered to imagine a big red stop sign. Then I said "Stop!" to myself. That helped me to calm down.**

Teacher: **That's great! Did you take any deep breaths and blow out your anger?**

Scruff: **Oh! I knew there was something I forgot.**

Teacher: **That's O.K., Scruff. It sounds like just imagining a stop sign and thinking "Stop!" to yourself was enough to help you calm down that time.**

Scruff: **Yeah. I stopped myself from throwing a Nintendo game at him!**

Teacher: **I'm glad the "stop" step helped you, Scruff. Sometimes cooling down is all that is needed to stop an argument from turning into a big fight. But sometimes it's not. Scruff, I've got another trick for you. It's called the "think" step. Why don't you sit over here while I tell you and the class about it?** *Find a place for Scruff to sit while you talk with the class about the "think" step.*

INTRODUCING THE "THINK" STEP

**Lesson 1,
Transp. #2
Transp. #1**

Put Transparency #2 from Lesson 1, "STP Traffic Light," on the overhead again. Say: **Once you've managed to cool down and get in control of your anger, you're able to go on to the next step, the "think" step.** *Point to the yellow circle on the traffic light.* **Just like when you see a yellow traffic light, you need to pause and think of the best thing to do.** *Show Transparency #1, "The Think Step."* **You need to ask yourself: "Should I walk away or stay?"**

You think to yourself, Is the smart thing to walk away, or should I stay and work this out? For instance, if a kid twice your size is bugging you, the smart thing would be to walk away, right? But if your best friend wants to play with the same toy that you do, you might decide the smart thing would be to stay and work it out with your friend. This lesson will teach you how to figure out whether the smart thing would be to walk away or stay in a conflict situation.

PRACTICING THE THINK STEP

Let's begin by practicing the "think" step together. Imagine that you're having an argument with a friend. You calm yourself down before you get <u>really</u> mad by imagining a big red stop sign *(pause)*, by saying "Stop!" to yourself *(pause)*, and by taking a deep breath and blowing out your anger *(model)*. Now we are going to think out loud. Repeat after me, "What's the smart thing to do—walk away or stay?" *Allow student repetitive response.*

Good! Let's see if you can remember this "think" question without having the overhead on. O.K., here we go! You're in an argument with a friend. You <u>stop</u> yourself and cool down. Now you <u>think</u> what? *Allow for student response: What's the smart thing to do— walk away or stay?*

DECIDING WHETHER TO WALK AWAY OR STAY

Transp. #2

Show Transparency #2, "The Big Question: Walk Away or Stay?" Keep the bottom half of the transparency covered. **The big question is: How do you know whether to walk away or stay when you are in a conflict or argument? Well, there are two answers to this question.** *Uncover and read answer #1:* **Walk away if you could get hurt.** *Next uncover and read answer #2:* **Walk away if you could get in trouble.**

If you're in danger of getting physically hurt by someone or of getting your feelings hurt, then you should walk away. If you're too mad to think straight and might do something that you'll be sorry about later, then you should walk away. In other words, you

should walk away if you might get hurt or get yourself in trouble. So, when should you walk away? *Encourage whole-group response.* **That's right. You should walk away if you might get hurt or get yourself in trouble. I think you've got it!**

MORE WORK WITH THE THINK STEP

Puppet

Put Scruff on your hand. Say: **Let's practice using the "think" step with Scruff.** *(To Scruff)* **Let's pretend that you are playing on some playground equipment. A big kid comes up to you and yells at you to get off the equipment. You calm yourself down by saying "Stop!" to yourself.** *(To class)* **What should Scruff ask himself first?**

Transp. #1

Allow for student response. Prompt students if they need help by pointing to the words on Transparency #1.

Try asking yourself that, Scruff.

Scruff: **O.K. What's the smart thing to do—walk away or stay?**

Transp. #2

Teacher: *(To Scruff)* **Great, Scruff!** *(To class)* **Now, class, how can Scruff decide whether he should walk away or stay?** *Point to the two answers on Transparency #2 and solicit group response.* **That's right! He needs to figure out if he could get hurt or get in trouble if he stayed.** *(To Scruff)* **So, Scruff, what are you going to figure out?**

Scruff: **Uh. If I will get hurt or will get in trouble?**

Teacher: **That's right, Scruff. Is there a chance you could get hurt?**

Scruff: **Yup! There sure is! That kid's really big. I think I'd better get out of there!**

Teacher: **Good thinking, Scruff! The smart thing to do is to walk away if you might get hurt. Let's do one more quick role-play. Let's say that a kid who always puts you down comes over and starts calling you "stupid." You feel your muscles tighten and your hands making fists. You think of a stop sign and say "Stop!" to yourself, and you take a** deep breath. All you can hear is your brain saying, "Punch this kid. That'll make him stop!" Then you remember to think about what the smart thing to do would be. And you ask yourself, "Will I get myself in trouble if I stay?" *(To the class)* What should Scruff ask himself? *(Will I get myself in trouble if I stay?)* Is it possible that he could get himself in trouble? *Allow for student response. (To Scruff)* Sounds like you'd better ask yourself if you could get in trouble if you stay, Scruff.

Scruff: Am I going to lose my temper and get myself in trouble here?

Teacher: What do you think, Scruff? Your face is getting redder and redder.

Scruff: I think I'd better split. This kid drives me nuts. I'm losing it.

Teacher: Good thinking, Scruff! It's smart to walk away instead of getting yourself in trouble!

PRACTICE WITH SCENARIOS

Give each student a piece of blank paper. On one side have the students write a W for "walk away" and on the other side write an S for "stay." Tell the students that you are going to read some situations out loud. They are to think about whether the smart thing to do would be to walk away or stay. Have them hold up the W side of their paper if they think they should walk away and the S side if they think they should stay. After each scenario ask the students the reason for their vote, reminding them of the two questions regarding getting hurt or getting in trouble. Accept all rationales for responses but emphasize the obvious response.

Addie and Lina had always played together at recess, but then Lina made a new friend and wanted to play with her instead of with Addie. This was making Addie really mad. One day when Lina and her new friend were playing on the bars, Addie was so jealous that she felt like pushing the other girl off the bars. Should Addie walk away or stay? Hold up either the W or the S side of your paper. *Addie should probably walk away because she could lose her temper and get in trouble if she stays.*

Barnie borrowed Andre's baseball cards. When he returned them, there were several missing. When Andre asked him about it, Barnie said he didn't know what happened to them and acted like he could care less. Andre told Barnie that he was really mad. So Barnie said, "Well, what can I do? I don't know where they are." Should Andre walk away or stay and talk with Barnie about it? *Andre should probably stay and talk about it.*

Aldo is a strong boy who likes to go fast when he's going down the slide and also when he's going up the stairs of the slide. Tara likes to go down the slide, too, but not too fast. Every time Aldo gets behind Tara he pushes her so that she goes down the slide really fast. Tara's afraid she's going to get hurt. Should she walk away or stay? *Tara should probably walk away.*

Rupert and Casper live next door to each other. Rupert has a small trampoline. It's big enough for only one kid to jump at a time. Both boys like to use it. Rupert has a hard time sharing, and sometimes he doesn't keep his promise that he'll let Casper jump after 5 minutes are up. Casper tells Rupert three times that it's his turn, but Rupert just ignores him. Casper feels himself getting madder and notices he's yelling and his fists are clenched. He feels like knocking Rupert off the trampoline. Should he walk away or stay? *Casper should probably walk away until he can calm down.*

ROLE-PLAYING THE SCENARIOS

To give students practice using the "stop" and "think" steps, ask volunteers to role-play the scenarios above with you. For each scenario, have a student play the character who needs to make a smart choice—to walk away or to stay—while you take the other role. Prompt the student through the "stop" and "think" steps as necessary by saying things like, "What else could you do to calm down?" "What do you need to ask yourself?" "Could you get hurt?" "Could you blow up and get yourself in trouble?" "Should you walk away or stay?" Ask students to think "out loud" as they go through the steps.

REVIEW AND LOOK AHEAD

Let's review what we've been learning about the STP approach for handling conflicts. *Review by asking these questions.*

- **What does the S stand for?**

- **What are some things you can do to stop yourself from escalating a conflict?**

- **What does the T stand for?**

- **What's the first question you should ask yourself?**

- **When should you walk away instead of staying?**

| Handout #1 |

Give students Handout #1, "The Think Step," and hang the poster with the same title where all students can easily refer to it. Say: **I'd like you to practice what we've been learning. A few times each day, look at the posters I've hung in the room or the handouts you've received and say the "stop" and "think" steps to yourself. When we have our next lesson I'll be drawing your names and asking students to come up and tell the class either the "stop" step or the "think" step. You can use Scruff to tell the class the steps if you wish. But be sure you know them!**

| Transp. #3/ Handout #2 |

During the week, watch for a time when you or some else is involved in a disagreement and should stop and think, "What's the smart thing to do here? Should I walk away or stay?" The conflict could be at home or in your neighborhood, in our classroom, or on the playground. Without using any names, you can tell us about the conflict you saw during our next lesson. As a class we'll decide if the person should have walked away or stayed. *Show and give students Transparency #3/Handout #2, "I Can Stop and THINK," as a homework assignment. Go over the directions with the class.*

Continue by saying: **Another thing I would like for you to do this week is help each other with the "stop" and "think" steps. When you see a classmate in an argument, remind him or her in a kind way to use the "stop" and "think" steps. You can do this by whispering something to the person like, "Remember the stop sign" or "Don't forget to stop and think." Or, if the conflict is occurring in our classroom, you could just point to the STOP and THINK posters as a reminder. Don't give these reminders in a bossy way, because nobody likes a bossy person.**

When we are learning something new we all need help. But usually people will accept help only from people they think care about them. So if you don't like a kid or may embarrass him or her by saying something, it's better not to say anything. And remember, no ganging up on anyone! The idea is to give a <u>reminder</u> in a nice way to help the other person use the "stop" and "think" steps. Only remind kids <u>once</u>, and if you get a reminder from someone this week, just say "thanks." Don't let it embarrass you. Tell yourself, "I'm just human" or "They're supposed to remind me." Remind yourself that everyone needs help practicing something new.

When we start our next lesson, we'll see how all of you did with using the "stop" and "think" steps when you got into disagreements. Then we'll learn the next step: Pick a Plan. That's the green light in STP. We'll talk about plans for when you decide the smart thing is to walk away from a conflict. In other lessons we'll talk about plans for when you decide to stay and resolve the conflict.

Summarize the lesson by asking students to complete the following lesson stems for review:

- **I learned ...**

- **A way I can use what I learned is ...**

- **STP is sort of like ...**

SUPPLEMENTARY ACTIVITIES

Use the supplementary activities that follow this lesson to reinforce the lesson concepts.

- *Stop and Think Tic-Tac-Toe*
  (Supplementary Activity #1)

- *Help Scruffy "Think" Smart*
  (Supplementary Activity #2)

- *Smart Thinking*
  (Supplementary Activity #3)

- *The STP Game*
  (Supplementary Activity #4)

TRANSPARENCY #1/HANDOUT #1/POSTER

The **T**hink Step

TRANSPARENCY #2

The Big Question:
Walk Away or Stay?

QUESTION

How do you know whether to WALK AWAY or STAY?

ANSWER

1. **Walk away if you could get HURT.**

2. **Walk away if you could get in TROUBLE.**

TRANSPARENCY #3/HANDOUT #2

I Can Stop and THINK

1. Which question should you ask yourself at the "think" step? Check (✓) one of the questions below.

    ❏ How can I get even?
    ❏ If I fight will I get caught?
    ❏ Should I walk away or stay?
    ❏ Should I hit this kid?
    ❏ Should I tattle?

2. Write the question in the bubble.

3. Color the picture below to make it look like you.

SUPPLEMENTARY ACTIVITY #1

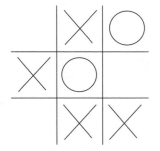

Stop and Think
Tic-Tac-Toe

Read the sentence in each box. Decide if it is true or false. Mark the box with an **X** if the sentence is true and an **O** if it is false. You can mark the **X** or **O** on top of the words. Did you get a tic-tac-toe? You can get one!

Saying or thinking "Stop!" can help you to stop a small problem from turning into a big one.	It is not normal to have disagreements with others.	If someone is bigger or stronger than you and is trying to hurt you, the smart thing to do is walk away.
When you are having an argument with someone, you should think, "If I fight this kid can I win?"	Even good friends have disagreements.	The "S" in STP stands for "Start."
It is smart to walk away from a disagreement with someone if you are so mad that you will get yourself in trouble if you stay.	The "T" in STP stands for "Talk."	It will make an argument worse if you take a deep breath and blow out your anger.

SUPPLEMENTARY ACTIVITY #2

Help Scruffy "Think" Smart

A big bully is picking on Scruffy. Help Scruffy decide whether the smart thing to do is to **walk away and get help from someone** or **stay and try to ignore the bully**. Take Scruffy through the maze to the right answer.

Stay
and try to
ignore the bully

Walk away
and get help

START

SUPPLEMENTARY ACTIVITY #3

Smart Thinking

When is it smart for you to walk away from an argument?
Use the code below to find the answer.

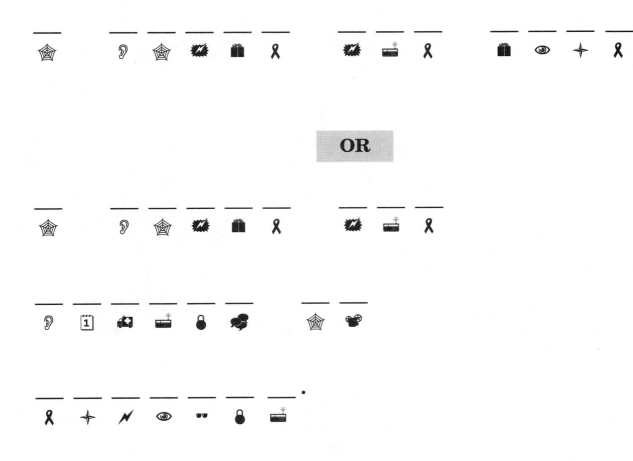

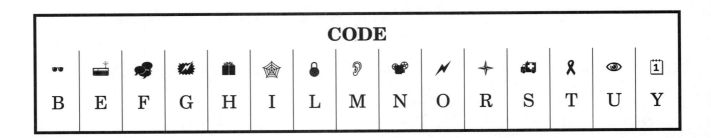

SUPPLEMENTARY ACTIVITY #4

The STP Game

(Phases 1 and 2)

Objective   Students will review and practice the "stop" and "think" steps through participation in an STP simulation game.

Materials   Big beach ball

Large traffic light poster
(see Supplementary Activity #4 Teacher Sheet for instructions on making the poster)

Student/teacher generated situation cards

Whistle

Procedure   This STP game will be taught in two parts. Phases 1 and 2, taught in this activity, will help students to review and practice the "stop" and "think" STP steps. Phase 3 will be added in Lesson 6 after the students have been introduced to all aspects of the "pick a plan" step.

Prepare the traffic light for the STP simulation game by following the directions on Supplementary Activity #4 Teacher Sheet "Large Traffic Light Poster Instructions." You will also need to prepare the situation cards by brainstorming "conflict situations" with the class. Write each conflict situation students suggest on a 3" x 5" card. Cards will include such things as, "I was in line to get a drink and another student pushed in ahead of me." You may also wish to use some of the situations suggested in Lesson 3, Supplementary Activity #3, and Lesson 4, Supplementary Activity #2. (In preparation for Phase 3 of the game to be played after Lesson 6, continue to add to the "situation cards" as new conflicts arise or come to mind.)

To play the game, students may either sit in a circle or be seated at their desks. The directions for phases 1 and 2 follow.

PHASE 1

Attach the red light to the poster. Instruct students to throw the beach ball to one another at random around the circle or classroom. When the "traffic attendant" (either you or a student appointed by you) blows the whistle, the activity stops. The student who has the ball draws a situation card. After reading the card read out loud, the student must state what he or she should do at the "stop" step to stop the problem from getting worse. Once stated, play continues until the whistle is blown again and another student gets to pick a card and state what he or she should do at the "stop" step. Once students are proficient at stating behaviors used at the "stop" step, the class may move to phase 2.

PHASE 2

Using the red and yellow lights, follow the game procedure described above. This time the "traffic attendant" will attach either the red or yellow light to the poster before he or she blows the whistle. The student who has the ball when the whistle is blown draws a situation card. After reading the card aloud, the student must state what he or she should say or think at the step indicated by the traffic light.

Once the ball is in play again, the "traffic attendant" may keep the traffic light on the same color or change it before blowing the whistle again. Make sure the game keeps moving by not allowing too much time between light changes and whistle blows.

Large Traffic Light Poster Instructions

Materials   1 piece of poster board

1 piece each of red, yellow, and green construction paper

Compass

Plasti-Tak

Black marker

Transparency #2 from Lesson 1, "STP Traffic Light"

Directions

1. Using the STP traffic light from Transparency #2 in Lesson 1 as a pattern, draw an STP traffic light on a piece of poster board. Use a compass to make the three traffic light circles.

2. Cut a red, yellow, and green circle out of construction paper, using a compass to draw the circles the same size as the ones on the poster.

3. Write the word STOP on the red circle with a black marker.

4. Write the word THINK on the yellow circle with a black marker.

5. Write the word PLAN on the green circle with a black marker.

6. If possible, laminate the poster and three construction paper circles.

7. Put a piece of Plasti-Tak on the back of each of the construction paper circles.

Lesson 3

Stop, Think, and Pick a Plan— A Conflict Resolution Process

STEP 3: Pick a Plan
Walk Away and Get Help From Someone You Trust, Do Something Else, or Cool Down

<u>S</u>top, <u>T</u>hink, and Pick a <u>P</u>lan— A Conflict Resolution Process

STEP 3: Pick a Plan
Walk Away and Get Help From Someone You Trust, Do Something Else, or Cool Down

Objective   Students will learn to walk away and seek help from someone they trust, engage in another activity, or use an anger reduction strategy to avoid escalation of a conflict.

Materials   Transparency #2 from Lesson 1 – "STP Traffic Light"

Transparency #1/Handout #1 – "The Pick a <u>P</u>lan Step (What to Do If You <u>Walk Away</u>)"

Transparency #2 – "What to Do When You Walk Away From a Conflict"

Transparency #3/Handout #2 – "Go Do Something Else"

Transparency #4/Handout #3 – "Take Time to Cool-Down"

"Cool-Down Idea" Cards (cut from the Teacher Resource page and placed in a basket)

Handout #4 – "A Way I Like to Cool Myself Down When I'm Angry"

Scruffy the STP Dog puppet from Lesson 1

Poster #1 – "The Pick a <u>P</u>lan Step"

Poster #2 – "Take Time to Cool-Down"

Poster #3 – "Do Something Else"

Poster #4 – "Get Help"

To the Teacher

This lesson gives students some strategies for de-escalating a conflict situation when they make the decision to walk away from the conflict rather than staying in it. Students will learn that there is a distinction between talking to someone they trust about a conflict and tattling and that it's appropriate to get help if they are in a conflict in which they might get hurt.

Getting help, however, is not appropriate for every conflict situation. Students will learn that, sometimes, leaving the situation and engaging in a different activity is the wise thing to do. Through a brainstorming exercise, students will broaden their repertoire of alternate games and activities.

Students will also learn the stragegy of taking time to cool down when they walk away from a conflict. Students need to employ this strategy when the "stop" step isn't enough and they are in danger of losing control and getting themselves in trouble. As part of this strategy students will learn two basic principles for managing their anger and will consider a wide array of options that can facilitate the use of these principles. Then they will play a pantomime game to practice cool-down activities.

At the end of this lesson, we recommend that you display the posters that reinforce the lesson concepts in a place where students will be able to use them as a reminder for the rest of the week.

Lesson Presentation

REVIEW OF PREVIOUS LESSONS

Since our last lesson, how many of you saw someone having an argument, either in real life or on TV? *Allow for student response.* **Did anyone see a TV character use the "stop" and "think" steps?** *Allow for response.* **When you get good at using STP you are going to be way ahead of a lot of adults. Most adults have never learned how to slow down, control their tempers, and think of the smart thing to do.**

You now know that conflicts are a normal part of life. Everyone has them! What you may not realize is that conflicts can give us the opportunity to learn how to get along with others better. So conflicts shouldn't be looked at as being all-bad. Raise your thumbs if you had a disagreement with someone this past week. Did anybody remember to use any parts of the "stop" and "think" steps? *Allow for student response.* **Don't be upset if you didn't use the "stop" and "think" steps. It takes a lot of practice to remember to stop and think when you're mad.**

Ask students to get out their STP folders, find their homework page, "I Can Stop and THINK," and show their paper to a learning partner or others in their group. Then put Transparency #2 from Lesson 1, "STP Traffic Light," on the overhead. Explain to the class that you are going to draw names at random (using Popsicle sticks with the students' names on them). Ask the students whose names are drawn to tell the class the things they should do in the "stop" step or the questions they should ask themselves in the "think" step. You may want to give students the option of using Scruff to "say" the "stop" and "think" steps.

INTRODUCTION TO THE PICK A PLAN STEP

Transp. #1

Great! I think you all now know the importance of cooling down, getting in control of your anger, and thinking about whether the smart thing to do is to walk away or stay when you're in a conflict or argument. You're now ready to learn the final step in the STP process—"Pick a Plan." *Put Transparency #1, "The Pick a Plan Step (What to Do If You Walk Away)," on the overhead.* **This is the step where you decide what to do after you choose either to walk away or stay.** *Point to the "stay" side of the transparency and say:* **Later on you'll be learning five things you can do if you decide to stay in a conflict situation. In this lesson, we'll be focusing on what to do if you decide the best thing is to walk away.**

By the end of this lesson, you'll know three plans you can use if you decide the smart thing is to walk away from a conflict. You can get help, you can go do something else, or you can take time to cool down. Which plan you use will depend on the situation. By the end of this lesson you'll know some ways that you can help yourself to feel better when you walk away from a conflict and to cool down when you're still really mad.

GET HELP

Transp. #2

Show Transparency #2, "What to Do When You Walk Away From a Conflict." Cover the lower two thirds of the transparency. **Let's talk first about when getting help would be the best thing to do. Let's say that your class is doing an art project and the kid next to you starts poking you with her scissors. You've told her several times**

to stop but she won't. In fact, she keeps poking harder and harder. This is a situation where you should talk to an adult. You need an adult to help you with this kid. In this case, do you think it's tattling to tell the teacher what's going on? *Allow for student response and ask students to support their answers. Then explain to the students that if someone is going to get hurt, it's not tattling to go to an adult for help. Explain that tattling is when you want to get a kid in trouble when you aren't in any danger.*

Here's another situation. Let's say that on your way to school an older kid tells you to give him your lunch money. You don't, and you run the rest of the way to school to get away from the kid. But he yells after you that he's going to get you after school and you'll be sorry. You feel frightened all day long. Finally you tell your teacher that you're afraid to walk home from school and the reason why. The teacher arranges for another student in class to walk with you. Was it tattling to tell her about the bully? *Allow for student response. Again, have students explain their reasoning.*

What are some other situations when it would be smart to get help from an adult? *Allow for student response.*

When you are in a conflict situation in which you are afraid that you will get hurt, you need to talk to someone you trust. Who are some people here at school you might talk with? Who are some people in your family or in your neighborhood? *List these people on the "Get help" part of the transparency.*

GO DO SOMETHING ELSE

Draw students' attention to the second strategy on Transparency #2, "What to Do When You Walk Away From a Conflict," leaving the third portion of the transparency covered. **Now let's talk about what you can do when you are in a conflict situation in which you've chosen to walk away but you are not in danger of being hurt. That would mean you're in danger of getting into trouble if you stay. In situations**

like this, it is not necessary to go to an adult with your problem. You're old enough to handle it yourself.

Let's say that there is a kid at recess who wants to play jump rope with some other kids. The other kids tell her she can't play because there are already too many kids playing. She asks them again but they still say "no," so she decides that the best thing to do is to walk away. Her feelings are hurt and she feels sad. What she needs to do is to go do something else. What she <u>doesn't</u> need to do is to stay and get upset. She also <u>doesn't</u> need to go tattle or try to get other kids mad at the jump ropers. What are some games or activities she could do so that she would have an O.K. recess? *Jot down student suggestions on the transparency. If students don't mention the following, you might add ideas like ask a peer who is alone if he or she would like to play, see if you can join a game that is going on like Four Square or kick ball, play on the bars or other playground equipment, see if there is any play equipment left that you could use alone like a jump rope or a ball to play wall ball, ask if you can read a book quietly in the library or classroom, ask the custodian if there are any jobs you can do, pick up litter, sit and count ants, look for interesting insects, think about things that make you happy.*

Transp. #3

Show students Transparency #3, "Go Do Something Else." Ask them to watch as you point to each of the seven pictures. Have them raise their hands when you point to a picture of something that they might like to do when they decide it's best to walk away from a conflict. Explain that you will give them a handout of this transparency at the end of the lesson and ask them to complete it for homework. Mention that as part of the assignment they'll be asked to draw a picture of themselves doing what would work the very best for them when they decide it would be smart to leave a conflict.

Transp. #2

Place Transparency #2, "What to Do When You Walk Away From a Conflict," back on the overhead. Point to the "Go do something else" box and say: **We've come up with some really good ideas here. You know, sometimes kids get into the habit of doing a certain thing at recess and they don't realize that there actually are a lot of other things they could do. The same thing is true when you're away from school. Sometimes it's smart to leave a conflict and think of** something else to do. Say you want to watch TV but your older brother is already watching his favorite program. Instead of making a big argument out of it, you can . . . *Have students say "Go do something else" as you point to the words on the transparency.* What are some things you could do if you were in this situation? *Allow for student response.*

TAKE TIME TO COOL DOWN

Draw students' attention to the third strategy on Transparency #2, "What to Do When You Walk Away From a Conflict." Let's suppose that you make the wise choice to leave a conflict. You've done the "stop" step: You've imagined the stop sign, said "Stop!" to yourself, and have taken some deep breaths. This worked well enough for you to be able to make the smart choice to leave the conflict. But you're still so mad about what happened that you can hardly stand it. You're not in danger of being hurt, so you don't need to talk to an adult about it. You're not in any mood to go join another game or play with anybody. What you need most is to take some time to cool down. *Point to those words on the transparency.*

A lot of kids, and adults too, don't know how to calm themselves down once they get really angry. They want to change the way they feel because anger is so uncomfortable, but they don't have a clue about what to do. Let's talk now about some good ways to get rid of the uncomfortable feeling you get when you're really, really angry.

**Transp. #4
Handout #3**

Show Transparency #4, "Take Time to Cool-Down," and give students the corresponding handout. Have them turn their papers over and focus on the overhead. Point to the box containing "The Two Best Cool-Down Secrets" and say: The most important things to remember to help you cool-down are (1) to stop thinking about what's making you angry and (2) to stop thinking about how to get even. These can be really hard to do. Some kids pretend that they are changing the channel of a TV to get these thoughts to go away. Other kids get busy doing something else. What might you do? *Allow for student discussion.*

When you're really mad, you need to get the anger out of your body. Some kids like to move to get the anger out of their bodies. Other kids like to do something quiet. Here are some things you can do at school or at home to cool-down. *Have students turn their papers so that the print side is up. Go over the left column of the list with the class. Say:* **These are things that kids can do to get the anger out of their arms and legs.** *As you read the items, ask the students to check or underline the techniques that they think would work best for them. Ask the students for other ideas and add them to the transparency. Point out that when students are doing any of these activities, especially activities such as squeezing clay or hitting a pillow, they* <u>should not</u> *pretend they are hurting the person they are angry with. This will only feed their anger.*

Now point to the right column of the list. Say: **These are some quieter activities that can also help you cool-down and feel better.** *As you read through the list, have the students again indicate on their handout the suggestions for cooling down that they particularly like. Ask the students for other ideas and add them to the list. Caution the students that "calling somebody on the phone" doesn't mean trying to align other students against the person they've had the conflict with.*

After you have gone through the list with the students, go through it again and have them raise their hands when you read an item they have checked or underlined. Take a hand count for each item and write the number on the transparency. Discuss the results with the students, pointing out that there are no right or wrong ways to cool down. Everybody has his or her own way.

COOL-DOWN PANTOMIME GAME

Let's play a game to practice some of the cool-down activities we have talked about. *Prepare ahead of time the "Cool-Down Idea" cards (cut from the Teacher Resource page) and place them in a basket.* **In this basket are some pieces of paper with some cool-down activities written on them. I'm going to draw a Popsicle stick and if your name is on it, you get to draw a card and hand it to me. I'll whisper to you which cool-down idea is written on the card you drew. Then your job is to act out, or pantomime, the cool-down idea. You can't**

say anything. The rest of the class will try to guess which cooling-off idea you're acting out. They'll raise their hands if they think they know, and you can call on someone. If the person guesses right, he or she gets to do the next pantomime. Don't call on anybody who has already come up and done a pantomime. *Have the students play the game until all the cards are drawn or an allotted amount of time is up.*

PICK A PLAN PRACTICE

Transp. #1

Show Transparency #1, "The Pick a Plan Step (What to Do If You Walk Away)." Point to the three plans on the overhead as you mention them to the class. **You've learned three plans you can use to help you feel better if you decide to walk away from a conflict: You can get help; you can go do something else; or you can take time to cool-down. Each of these plans can be used for different kinds of problems whenever you think that the best thing to do is walk away.**

Puppet

Put Scruffy on your hand and have him greet the class.

Teacher: **Scruffy, I know you're kind of shy talking about times when you and your friends have conflicts. But I also know that there were three times this past week when you did the smart thing and walked away from a conflict. We've just been studying three plans that are good to use when you walk away from a conflict. Would it be O.K. if I told the kids about the three situations that you walked away from and then let them tell you what they think you could have done next?**

Scruff: **It's O.K. with me if you want to tell them. But why do I have to know what to do next? I was smart enough to leave, wasn't I?**

Teacher: **It was good that you left, Scruff, and I'm really proud of you for doing that. But after you decide to walk away from a situation, you still have to pick a plan for what you're going to do next.**

Scruff: **Yes, I guess I do.**

Teacher: *(To the class)* **As I tell you about the predicaments Scruffy walked away from, I want all of you to think about which of the three plans we just learned would have worked best to help Scruff solve the conflict.**

Read the following scenarios to the class. After reading each one, select a student at random (by using the Popsicle stick method) to state what Scruff could have done next.

Scruffy and a friend were playing hopscotch during recess. His friend kept stepping on the lines but saying that he wasn't. Scruff tried to talk with his friend about it but he still kept cheating. Finally Scruffy decided that the best thing to do was to walk away, since it was no fun playing hopscotch with someone who was cheating. Once he walked away from the hopscotch game, what should he have done next? Should he have (1) gotten help from an adult; (2) done something else; or (3) taken time to cool-down? Why? *(He should have gone to do something else.)*

Scruff and some friends were riding bikes in their neighborhood. One of the kids Scruffy was playing with decided it would be fun to throw rocks at Scruff's bike as he rode by. Scruffy told him to stop, but he just laughed and called Scruff a "scaredy cat." Scruffy decided that the best thing to do was to stop riding his bike and get away from the kid who was throwing rocks because Scruff knew this was dangerous and he could get really hurt. What would have been a good plan for Scruffy to pick in this situation? Why? *(Get help.)*

Scruffy and his friend, Monty, began comparing the new shoes they both had. They started arguing about whose sneakers were better. Both Scruff and Monty got angrier and angrier. Scruff tried to take deep breaths and cool-down, but then Monty started calling him names and that made Scruff even madder! He decided that the smart thing to do was to walk away because he was getting so mad he was about to punch Monty! What should Scruff

have done next? Why? *(He should have taken time to cool-down. Have the class tell Scruff some of their favorite ways to cool down.)*

Teacher: **Good job, class! What do you think, Scruff? Do you like these three plans for what to do when you walk away from a situation?**

Scruff: **Yeah, they're great! Now I know that if I'm afraid I'll get hurt, I need to get help. If my friend cheats at hopscotch again, I know that I don't need to tattle. Instead I'll find something else to do where I can have fun. And if I'm really mad, now I know there are a lot of things I can do to cool down! I think I'll try running around the school first. And if that doesn't work, I'll get some paper and draw to get my mind off it.**

Teacher: **Great, Scruffy! I think you've got it! Thanks, class, for helping Scruff learn about three good plans for handling disagreements. You did a great job! Bye, Scruff. See you later!**

Scruff: **Bye, everybody.**

REVIEW AND HOMEWORK

**Lesson 1,
Transp. #2
Transp. #1**

We've talked about a lot today! Let's go over what we've talked about really quickly. *Show Transparency #2 from Lesson 1, "STP Traffic Light."* **Remember, first you STOP, then you THINK if it's smart to walk away or stay, and then you PICK A PLAN. I told you at the beginning of this lesson that by the end of the lesson you would know some helpful things to do when you walk away from a conflict. Who can remember one of the three plans we talked about?** *Allow for student responses. Then put Transparency #1, "The Pick a Plan Step (What to Do If You Walk Away)" on the overhead and have the class read it together. Review the lesson by asking the following questions:*

- **When should you get help with a conflict?**

- **What is the difference between tattling and going to an adult for help?**

- **What are some games or activities you can do when you leave a conflict?**

- **When is it good to take time to cool down when you leave a conflict?**

- **What are the two best cool-down secrets?**

- **What are some of the cool-down tricks we talked about?**

Pass out Handout #2, "Go Do Something Else," and Handout #4, "A Way I Might Like to Cool Myself Down When I'm Angry." Read the directions to the students and ask them to complete the handouts by the next lesson.

SUPPLEMENTARY ACTIVITIES

Use the supplementary activities that follow this lesson to reinforce the lesson concepts.

- *STP Crossword Puzzle
  (Supplementary Activity #1)*

- *Walk Away Plan Scramble
  (Supplementary Activity #2)*

- *What If?
  (Supplementary Activity #3)*

- *This Is a Picture of Me Walking Away From Trouble
  (Supplementary Activity #4)*

- *Take Time to Cool Down
  (Supplementary Activity #5)*

TRANSPARENCY #1/HANDOUT #1

The Pick a Plan Step
What to Do If You Walk Away

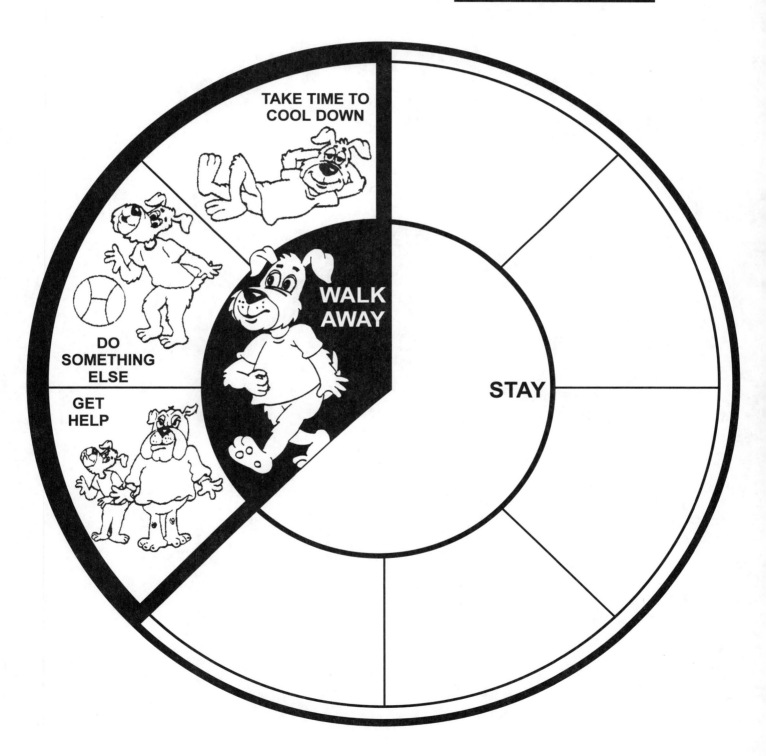

TAKE TIME TO
COOL DOWN

DO
SOMETHING
ELSE

GET
HELP

WALK
AWAY

STAY

TRANSPARENCY #2

What to Do When You Walk Away From a Conflict

You can:

Get help.

Go do something else.

Take time to cool down.

TRANSPARENCY #3/HANDOUT #2

Go Do Something Else

1. Circle the pictures below that represent things you might like to do on the playground if you decide to walk away from a conflict.
2. In the empty box draw yourself doing something that would be fun and would help you feel better after you have walked away from a conflict.

TRANSPARENCY #4/HANDOUT #3

Take Time to Cool-Down

The Two Best Cool-Down Secrets:

1. Stop thinking about what's making you angry.

2. Stop thinking about how to get even.

Cool-Down Tricks:

- ❏ Ride a bike
- ❏ Run around the block or play-ground
- ❏ Jump rope
- ❏ Lift weights
- ❏ Stamp your feet
- ❏ Jump on a trampoline
- ❏ Push against a wall
- ❏ Do jumping jacks
- ❏ Hit a pillow
- ❏ Go outside and play
- ❏ Count to ten
- ❏ Squeeze clay

- ❏ Draw or doodle
- ❏ Play computer games
- ❏ Read
- ❏ Write a story
- ❏ Play with your pet
- ❏ Talk to someone
- ❏ Hug or talk to a stuffed animal
- ❏ Watch TV
- ❏ Take a nap
- ❏ Call somebody on the phone
- ❏ Listen to music
- ❏ Think about things that make you happy

- ❏ Your ideas

TEACHER RESOURCE

COOL-DOWN IDEA CARDS

Ride a bike	Play with your pet
Jump rope	Watch TV
Run around	Take a nap
Do jumping jacks	Push against a wall
Lift weights	Listen to music
Stamp your feet	Think about things that make you happy
Go outside and play	Hug or talk to a stuffed animal
Call somebody on the phone	Hit a pillow
Play computer games	Talk to someone
Jump on a trampoline	Write a story
Count to ten	Squeeze clay
Draw or doodle	Read

HANDOUT #4

A Way I Might Like to Cool Myself Down When I'm Angry

1. **Circle one thing that you might like to do to cool-down when you are angry.**

play with your pet

talk to someone

count to ten

hug or talk to a stuffed animal

write a story

squeeze clay

jump rope

go outside and play

ride a bike

think about things that make you happy

read

jump on a trampoline

stamp your feet

draw or doodle

play computer games

watch TV

run around

listen to music

push against a wall

hit a pillow

lift weights

do jumping jacks

call somebody on the phone

2. **Draw a picture of yourself doing the activity you have circled.**

POSTER #1

The Pick a <u>P</u>lan Step

POSTER #2

Take Time to Cool-Down

POSTER #3

Do Something Else

POSTER #4

Get Help

SUPPLEMENTARY ACTIVITY #1

STP
Crossword Puzzle

Using the hints below, fill in the boxes with the correct letters to make some STP words. (The word list at the bottom will also help you!)

ACROSS

1. When you try to join a game but kids say you can't play, sometimes the best thing to do is walk away and do _____ else.
2. If a bully is picking on you, you should go find a person you _____ to help you.
3. If you are really mad at a friend and are going to get yourself in trouble if you stay, the best thing to do is walk away and take time to _____ down.
4. The "P" in the STP steps stands for "Pick a _____."

DOWN

1. In the "think" step of STP you ask yourself: "Should I walk away or _____?"
2. If you are having a disagreement with another kid and it looks like you could get hurt, you should walk away and get _____.
3. Get help from someone you trust, do something else, and take time to cool down are three things you can do if you decide that the smart thing to do in a conflict is _____ away.

WORD LIST

stay   cool   help   pick   plan   someone   something   trust   walk

Walk Away Plan Scramble

Scruffy is trying to remember the three things that he can do when he gets in an argument and decides that the smart thing to do is walk away. He knows the three plans are written below, **but** the words for the plans are all mixed up! Unscramble the words for Scruffy so that he can pick a plan.

1. **from help get you someone trust**

    _____

    _____

    _____

2. **else do something**

    _____

    _____

    _____

3. **down take to cool time**

    _____

    _____

    _____

What If?

Objective   Students will gain practice in deciding when they should walk away from a conflict and what to do when they walk away.

Materials   Supplementary Activity #3 Teacher Sheet, "What If? Situations Cards" (cut the cards apart and put them in a basket)

Supplementary Activity #3 Transparency, "What If?"

Basket

Procedure   Instruct all of your students to hold up one, two, three, or four fingers. Have a volunteer draw a situation card from the basket. Read the number on the card and instruct all students holding up that number of fingers to stand. Read aloud the situation on the card. Using the discussion sheet transparency "What If," ask a standing student, "What if you walk away? What might happen? What might you do?" Record the student's answer in the appropriate column. Then ask another student, "What if you don't walk away in this situation? What might happen?" Invite more student responses from those standing and record the answer(s).

Next, instruct students to hold up a number of fingers corresponding to one of the three remaining situation cards. Proceed as with the first card drawn. Continue drawing situation cards and recording answers until all scenarios have been discussed. (For the last scenario, tell students that anyone in the class may offer an answer.)

SUPPLEMENTARY ACTIVITY #3 TEACHER SHEET

What If? Situation Cards

1

A boy in your class keeps tripping you in the halls and running into you at recess. Then he calls you "clumsy" and says, "Why don't you watch where you are going?" One day at recess he trips you again and won't leave you alone.

2

At your school there's a rule that after the first 5 minutes of recess no one can join the kick ball game. You decide that since you can't join the game, you could be the umpire. But the kids playing the game don't want an umpire.

3

You and the kid you're playing with are having a big argument over whose turn it is on the bars. The kid calls you a name and you give a worse put-down back. Your voices are getting louder and you feel your fingers tightening into fists.

4

Your best friend decides to play with someone else at recess. They don't want you playing with them. As you follow them around they start being mean to you and calling you names. You feel yourself getting really mad and you feel like throwing something at them.

SUPPLEMENTARY ACTIVITY #3 TRANSPARENCY

What If?

What if you walk away?	What if you don't?

SUPPLEMENTARY ACTIVITY #4

This Is a Picture of
Me Walking Away From Trouble

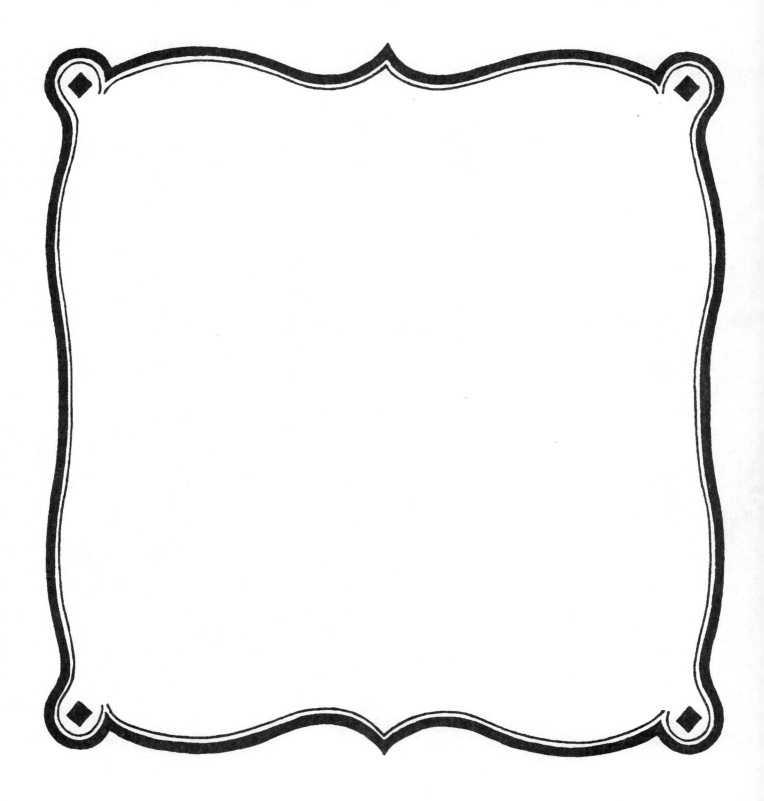

SUPPLEMENTARY ACTIVITY #5

Take Time to Cool Down

Copy the drawings in the squares below in the correct order on the grid.
Color the picture you make.

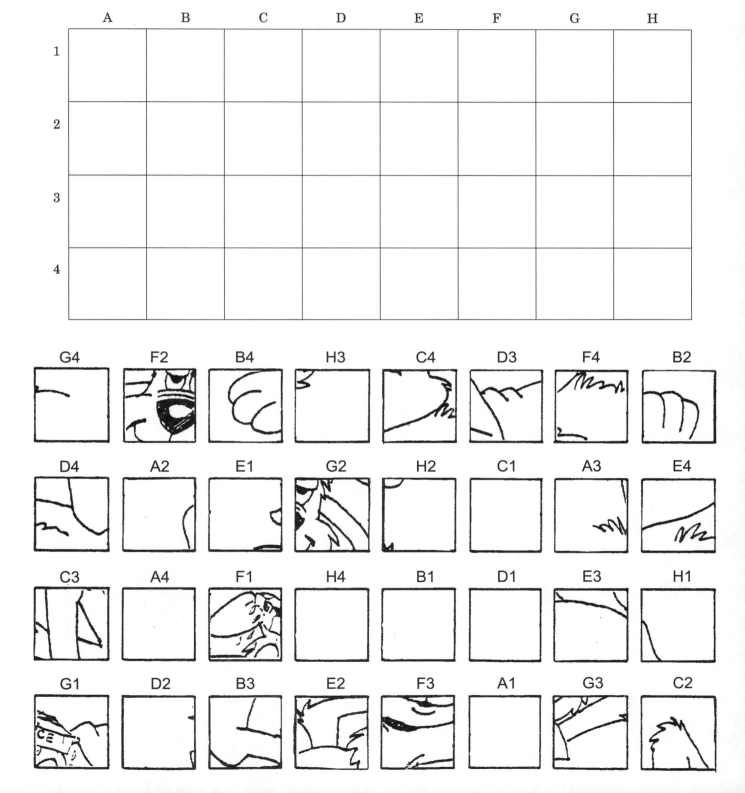

Lesson 4

**S̲top, T̲hink, and Pick a P̲lan—
A Conflict Resolution Process**

STEP 3: Pick a Plan
*Stay and Ignore It or
Say What You Want*

Stop, Think, and Pick a Plan—
A Conflict Resolution Process

STEP 3: *Pick a Plan*
Stay and Ignore It or Say What You Want

Objective   Students will learn the strategies of ignoring a provocation and telling the provoker what they want in a conflict situation.

Materials   Transparency #1 – "STP: Stop, Think, and Pick a Plan"

Transparency #1 from Lesson 3 – "The Pick a Plan Step (What to Do If You Walk Away)"

Transparency #2 – "The Pick a Plan Step (What to Do If You Stay)"

Transparency #3/Poster #1 – "Ignore It"

Transparency #4/Poster #2 – "Say What You Want"

Transparency #5 – "Tell Them to Stop"

Transparency #6/Handout #1 – "On the Watch for the 'Ignore It' and the 'Say What You Want' Plans"

Scruffy the STP Dog puppet from Lesson 1

To the Teacher

In this lesson students will begin to master some strategies to use when the wise thing to do is stay with the conflict situation and attempt to resolve it. The lesson focuses on situations in which a student is being provoked and teaches the strategies of ignoring a provocation and learning to tell someone what you want when you are being provoked. Both of these strategies call on students to utilize verbal and nonverbal assertiveness skills without displaying aggression. Students will work on these skills with the help of Scruffy the puppet and role-plays.

In addition to the role-plays suggested, you may want to brainstorm other role-play situations with your students. You'll have the greatest success in getting students to transfer the skills taught in this lesson to real life if you use role-play topics your class can relate to. At the end of this lesson, we recommend that you display the posters that reinforce the lesson concepts in a place where students will be able to use them as a reminder for the rest of the week.

Lesson Presentation

REVIEW OF PREVIOUS LESSONS

Transp. #1

Show Transparency #1, "STP: Stop, Think, and Pick a Plan." Cover the right side of the transparency so that only the traffic light is exposed. Tell the students that you are going to point to each of the lights and as you do so you would like them to shout out the main words on each: STOP, THINK, PICK A PLAN.

Lesson 3, Transp. #1

Say: **Now I'm going to ask you what's involved in each step. Who can tell me what's involved in the "stop" step?** *Ask for student volunteers. Then uncover the explanation of the "stop" step on the right side of the page and ask the entire class to read the explanation with you. Do the same thing for the "think" step. When you get to the "pick a plan" step, show Transparency #1 from Lesson 3, "The Pick a Plan Step (What to Do If You Walk Away)," and review the three plans to use when you've decided that walking away from a conflict is the best thing to do.* Ask: **Did any of you use any parts of the "stop," "think," and "pick a plan" steps since our last lesson?** *Allow for student response.*

OVERVIEW OF STAY STRATEGIES

We've just reviewed the three plans that work well in situations in which you decide it's best to walk away from a conflict. Now we're going to talk about some plans that work well when you decide it's best to stay and work out a conflict.

Transp. #2

Show students Transparency #2, "The Pick a Plan Step (What to Do If You Stay)." **Look up at the transparency and count the number of different plans you can choose from when you decide to stay to work out a conflict. Hold up your fingers to show how many plans there are. Right! There are five different plans. I'll read each one to you and you say them after me.**

You're going to get good at using all of these. In this lesson, you'll learn the powerful plans of ignoring the provocation and telling the person who's provoking you what you want. We'll go over the other plans in the next lesson.

"IGNORE IT" PLAN

Transp. #3

Show Transparency #3, "Ignore It." **Let's talk about times when you might just ignore a person or situation. The best time to use ignoring is when you know that a person wants to get you upset. Sometimes the best way to get people to stop doing what they're doing is to ignore them.**

For instance, suppose a kid makes a mean comment about a low grade you got on a spelling paper. This would be a good time to use the "ignore it" plan. Here's another situation: A kid tells you that what you are wearing looks weird. This would also be a good time to use the "ignore it" plan. Or suppose someone in your class keeps making tapping sounds with his pencil because he knows you don't like it. You'd probably be wise to decide to not waste your energy getting mad, but just to act like you don't hear it.

To use the "ignore it" plan so that it works, there are a few things that you need to know. First of all, you need to realize that you can be very powerful without saying anything. It all depends on the expression on your face and how you hold your body. You can't show that you're hurt or mad. Instead, you need to keep a calm expression on your face and hold your body really tall. I'll show you what I mean.

Puppet

I'll pretend that I'm a kid who just got a new haircut, and I want one of you to be Scruffy. *Call on a student volunteer to put on the Scruffy hand puppet. Explain that Scruffy thinks your new haircut looks really funny and keeps saying, "That haircut sure looks weird." Have the student say Scruffy's line. Model looking at the put-downer for a second and then just going back to what you were doing. Say to the class:* **Did you notice that I didn't act like my feelings were hurt or like I was upset? My face was calm the whole time. I stood tall and proud, and I just looked at Scruffy for a second and then I looked away and ignored him. The put-downer wanted to get me upset but he didn't get what he wanted, did he?**

Now I want all of you to try this technique. I'm going to give you a pretend put-down and I want you to look calm and powerful as

you look at me for a second and then look away and just ignore me. Ready? *Say:* **"You guys are the dumbest class I've ever had."**

Good job! When you gave me that calm, powerful look and then just looked away and ignored me, I felt like my put-down didn't bother you at all.

Ignoring definitely won't work if you look weak or hurt or like you're afraid of the person. I'll show you what I mean. *Call on another student to put on the Scruffy puppet and give you the same put-down about your haircut as before. This time, allow hurt and fear to register in your body stance and facial expression. After the role-play ask:* **Do you think this kind of ignoring works?** *Allow for student response.* **Why not?** *After students respond, say:* **That's right, the put-downer got what he wanted. He wanted to upset me, and he saw that I was upset even though I didn't say anything.**

Let's practice the "ignore it" plan. Pretend that you are working really hard on a math paper I've given you. Scruffy will go around and try to distract you by barking at you. If he comes to your desk, what will you do? *Allow for student response.* **That's right. Give him a calm, powerful look and then ignore him by going back to what you were doing.**

After the activity say: **Great job! Scruffy sure didn't get much attention, and he didn't seem to upset any of you.** *Look at Scruffy and say:* **Scruffy, do you want to keep trying to distract this class?**

Scruffy: **Nope. I give up. These kids act like they don't even care what I'm doing. That's no fun. I'll have to think of some other way to bug 'em!**

O.K., class. Who'd like to come up and practice the "ignore it" plan? We'll pretend Scruffy is a kid trying to bug you, tease you, or start an argument with you, and you can use the "ignore it" plan to stop him in his tracks. *Look at Scruffy and say:* **Do you mind doing this for us, Scruffy?**

Scruffy: **No, it's actually kind of fun to try to bug people. I sure hate it when I get ignored, though.**

Call on student volunteers. Use the Scruffy puppet to provide a variety of opportunities for them to ignore provocative behavior that leads to conflicts.

"SAY WHAT YOU WANT" PLAN

Transp. #4

You've done a great job using the "ignore it" plan! You do need to know that sometimes ignoring may not feel right to you. In those cases, there's another plan that a lot of kids have used and had good luck with. It's called the "Say What You Want" plan. *Show Transparency #4, "Say What You Want."*

Let's say that you have your favorite toy on a shelf in your room. You don't want anyone to play with it because it is so special to you. A friend of yours comes over to your house to play and takes your favorite toy off your shelf without asking. You don't want to ignore what your friend has done! You want your friend to know what you want.

When you tell another person what you want, the way you say it is very important. For instance, in the situation we just talked about, you <u>could</u> grab your toy from your friend's hands and say in a loud, rude tone, "Don't touch that!" or "Give me that! You can't play with that, you jerk!" How do you think your friend might feel then? *Allow for student response.* **That way of saying what you want wouldn't help the problem; instead, it would probably make things worse! You need to be strong but not rude.**

Point to the words "Be strong but not rude" on the transparency and read them to the students. Then say: **Instead of being rude, you could say to your friend in a kind but strong voice, "That's my favorite toy. I just got it and I don't want anyone to play with it. Please put it back." What do you think your friend might say?** *Allow for student response.* **That's right. He or she might just say something like, "Oh! O.K. Sorry!"**

Sometimes, when someone's doing something that bothers us, we have a strong urge to give a put-down or to blame the person. We might feel like saying, "You jerk!" or "You always wreck everything!" An easy way to keep yourself from giving a put-down or from blaming someone when you are saying what you want in a situation is to never start with the word "you." *Point to the transparency and read the statement, "Don't start with the word 'you.'"* **Let me show you what I mean. Let's say that somebody reaches into your desk and borrows your ruler without asking. You don't like people taking your things unless they ask you first. Listen to these different ways of telling the person what you want and raise your hand if the words I say would make you kind of mad.**

- **"Would you please ask me before you borrow my stuff?"**

- **"You always take my stuff!"** *(said in a rude way)*

- **"You creep! Who said you could get into my desk?"** *(said rudely)*

- **"I don't like it when you borrow my stuff without asking."**

- **"I'd like you to ask before you take my things."**

- **"You make me so mad!"** *(said in a rude way)*

Notice that when I started with "you" and was rude, it made more of you mad than when I started with the words in the thought bubbles. *Point to the two thought bubbles on the transparency.* **Telling someone what you would like by starting with the word "I" or "would" can help solve a problem rather than making it worse.**

I'd like you to practice this technique of telling someone what you want with your learning partner. Be sure to say what you want in a strong but not rude way. Those of you who are closest to the windows, pretend that you're the one who had the ruler taken without asking. Remember to say what you want in a way that will not make the other person mad but will help to solve the problem. Use the sentence starters on the transparency to help you think of what to say. Remember to not start with the word "you."

The rest of you pretend that you are the kid who has taken the ruler. Listen to what your partner says and see if his or her words would get you to stop and not make you mad. *Allow students time for this practice. Then have the students raise their thumbs if they felt it was easy to tell their partner what they wanted. Ask for volunteers to state their reaction to being told what their friend wanted.*

After the practice session, say: **Who can think of some other times when it might be good to tell someone what you want?** *Allow for student response. Have students practice one more time with their learning partners using one of these situations. This time have students trade roles so that the other student in the pair gets practice telling someone what he or she wants in a constructive manner.*

Continue the lesson by saying: **Saying what you want in a strong but not rude way can often stop small problems from turning into big ones. Many times, saying what you want will involve telling someone to <u>stop</u> what he or she is doing. Now, I'm sure that a lot of you have told kids who were bugging you to stop and it didn't work. Saying "stop" isn't magic, but there is a way that you can do it that sometimes gets results.**

Transp. #5

Show Transparency #5, "Tell Them to Stop." Have the steps covered, and reveal them one at a time as you go over them with the class. A sample script follows this paragraph. As you read the steps, model a firm tone of voice and put out your hand in a "Stop" motion each time you say "stop."

1. **Tell them to stop.**

   Model saying and motioning the word "stop." Explain: **If you say "stop" firmly enough, you may have to say it only once to get the other people to stop. But what do you do if they keep bugging you?** *Uncover the second step on the transparency.*

2. **Tell them again!**

    Explain: **You could say something like this (still using a firm voice): "I said, I don't like this. Stop!" And if this still doesn't work, there's one last thing you can say.** *Uncover the third step on the transparency.*

3. **"Last chance before I get an adult. I'm not going to get into a fight and get myself in trouble."**

    And if this doesn't work, do exactly what you said you'd do—leave and get an adult to help you take care of the problem. This way you won't get into trouble for fighting.

    Did you notice how strong my voice was without being bossy or mean? Did you notice that I put out my hand each time that I said "stop" to make my words sound stronger?

    Saying "stop" like this is a powerful way to let someone know you mean business! However, to do it right takes practice. *Ask for student volunteers to come to the front of the room and pretend that they are being provoked by another student. Take the role of the provoker yourself, doing irritating things you've seen happen between students in your classroom. During the role-plays, keep Transparency #5, "Tell Them to Stop," on the overhead so that the student volunteers can refer to it as they practice telling you to "stop." During some of the role-plays stop your behavior after the first or second time the student says "stop." In other role-plays continue provoking until the student says he or she will get an adult rather than get into a fight. In those cases, act like it isn't worth it to keep up the provocative behavior if the student refuses to fight back.*

    When the students have had sufficient practice, put Scruffy on your hand and say: **What do you think, Scruffy? Would this technique help you to stop an argument from turning into a fight?**

Scruffy: **I don't know. When I tell people to stop, they usually keep doing what they were doing, even though I say "please" just like you said to.**

Teacher: **Well, Scruffy, would you like to try this strategy once with me and see what happens?**

Scruffy: **Oh, I guess so. But it doesn't seem like this is a good strategy for me.**

Teacher: **Scruffy, why don't we practice together once before you give up? O.K.?**

Scruffy: *(reluctantly)* **O.K.**

Teacher: **Let's have a student come up and bug you by poking you. Has this ever happened to you?**

Scruffy: **Yeah! The kid who sits next to me at school does it all the time. I can never get her to stop. She thinks it's funny when I get upset.**

Teacher: **Well, Scruffy, let's see if we can help you learn to tell her to stop in a powerful way.** *Ask a girl in the class to come to the front of the room and begin gently poking Scruffy. Instruct her to continue poking Scruffy while he goes through all the "tell them to stop" steps. Prompt Scruffy in a whisper:* **O.K., Scruffy. Say "stop."**

Scruffy: *(In a whining, pleading voice)* **Stop.** *When this has no effect, have Scruffy continue, still using a whining voice, by saying:* **I said, stop it!** *As the student continues to poke Scruffy, have him state in a frantic voice:* **Last chance before I get an adult. I'm not going to get into a fight and get myself in trouble.**

Teacher: **Wait, Scruffy! You have all the words right. But listen to the sound of your voice! You have to say the words in a strong, powerful way. Who would like to show Scruffy how he needs to say these words so that he sounds like he means business?** *Allow for student response.* **Good job! Now, Scruffy, try it again and sound a little tougher, like you really mean it!**

Scruffy: **O.K.**

Teacher: **Remember, use your powerful and in-charge voice, not a whining, scared one. Sound firm and confident in what you say.** *Instruct a volunteer to once again start poking Scruffy. Have Scruffy tell the student to stop, but this time have Scruffy use a firm, confident voice. After Scruffy has finished, say:* **Much better, Scruffy!** *Ask the students to comment on the difference, stating what Scruffy did this time that would make this strategy work better.*

I think you're all really getting the hang of this! Remember, when you decide to tell someone to stop, make sure that you sound firm and confident, not bossy, mean, whining, or afraid. If you sound strong and confident, your words will have power and can actually get the person to stop what he or she is doing!

Now, I'd like all of you to practice the "tell them to stop" trick. *Divide the students into groups of two, designating one student in each pair as "Student A" and the other as "Student B." First have all of the students designated as "Student A" practice saying the statements on Transparency #5 to their partners. Then have the students reverse roles and go through the steps one more time.*

Following the practice say: **Hey, just for fun, let's pretend that this half of the room is bugging the other half of the room.** *Indicate an imaginary line down the middle of the room. Have all the students on the right side of the room tap their pencils on their desks. Lead the students on the left side of the room in saying in unison the three statements on the overhead. Then reverse the roles. Tell the provokers to decide if they want to stop after the first, second, or third statements.*

Summarize with: **You've got it! I see lots of you saying "stop" in a very powerful way! I hope the next time someone does something that you don't like, you'll try this "tell them to stop" trick to get them to stop bothering you.**

REVIEW AND HOMEWORK

Transp. #2

Once again show students Transparency #2, "The Pick a Plan Step (What to Do If You <u>Stay</u>)." **When you are in a conflict with someone and you decide that the smart thing to do is to stay, there are many things you can do to handle the disagreement. Today we talked about two of these plans: "ignore it" and "say what you want." Both of these are good plans to use if someone is upsetting you. Sometimes you might use one, and sometimes you might use the other.**

To help us review the plans we have learned today, I'm going to say or do some things that are meant to irritate you. I want you to decide if you will use the "ignore it" plan or the "say what you want" plan. If you decide to use the "ignore it" plan, give me a calm, cool look and then look away. If you decide to use the "say what you want" plan, put your hand to your mouth in a speaking motion. If you choose to ignore me and the person next to you chooses the "say what you want" plan, does that mean one of you is wrong? No! You'll probably all respond differently to each way I pretend to irritate you. Just pick the plan that feels right to you at the time.

Use the following provocations or brainstorm with your students to come up with others. Process the student responses after each scenario.

1. *"Hey, Clumsy. How many desks did you bump into today? Let's see you walk a straight line, Fumble Feet! Watch out, you might tip over."*

2. *Tell the students to imagine you're kicking their chairs as you kick a chair in the front of the room.*

3. *Tell the students to imagine you are bumping into them and mimic doing it.*

4. *Tell the students to imagine that you have taken something of theirs and are holding it really high in the air so they can't reach it while you say, "Come on, you can reach it. Just jump!"*

End the exercise by saying: **You've all done a terrific job of choosing the best plan for you when I was pretending to start a conflict.** *Then give the students Handout #1, "On the Watch for the 'Ignore It' and the 'Say What You Want' Plans." Show the students the transparency with the same title and go over directions, modeling how to use the worksheet as a tally sheet. Explain to the students that they will be keeping this handout on their desks during the week, keeping their tallies of times people use the plans. During the next lesson they will get to add up their totals for each area and share their findings.*

SUPPLEMENTARY ACTIVITIES

Use the supplementary activities that follow this lesson to reinforce the lesson concepts.

- *STP Spaghetti Message*
  (Supplementary Activity #1)

- *More Practice With the "Ignore It" Plan*
  (Supplementary Activity #2)

- *O.K. Ways to Tell Them to Stop*
  (Supplementary Activity #3)

- *STP Traffic Light*
  (Supplementary Activity #4)

TRANSPARENCY #1

STP: <u>S</u>top, <u>T</u>hink, and Pick a <u>P</u>lan

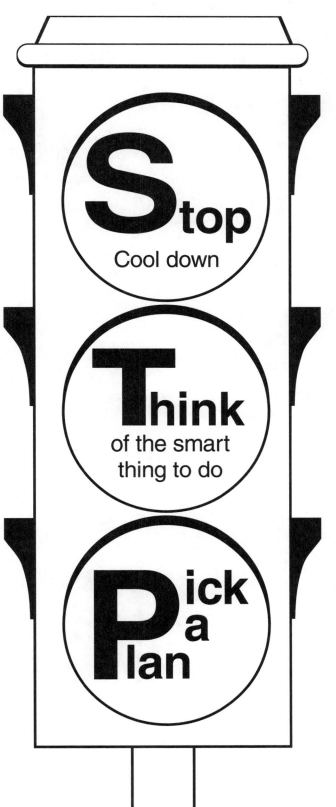

STOP
Think or say "Stop!"
Take a deep breath.

THINK
"What's the smart
thing to do:
walk away **or** stay?"

PICK a PLAN

If you walk away:	If you stay:
• Get help from someone you trust.	• Ignore it.
• Go do something else.	• Say what you want.
	• Make a deal (negotiate).
• Take time to cool down.	• Use chance.
	• Say you're sorry.

TRANSPARENCY #2

The Pick a <u>P</u>lan Step
What to Do If You <u>Stay</u>

TRANSPARENCY #3/POSTER #1

Ignore It

Give a strong, powerful look and then look away.

TRANSPARENCY #4/POSTER #2

Say What You Want

Be strong but not rude.
Don't start with the word "you."

TRANSPARENCY #5

Tell Them to Stop

1. Tell them to "stop"!

2. Tell them again!

3. Then say:
"Last chance before I get an adult. I'm not going to get into a fight and get myself in trouble."

TRANSPARENCY #6/HANDOUT #1

On the Watch for the "Ignore It" and the "Say What You Want" Plans

Be a detective. Be on the watch this week for times when you and others use the "ignore it" and the "say what you want" plans. Keep a tally of the times you see others or yourself using one of these plans in the boxes below each statement.

IGNORE IT

• Times I noticed others ignoring someone who bugged them.

Total _____

• Times I ignored someone who bugged me.

Total _____

SAY WHAT YOU WANT

• Times I heard others use the "say what you want" plan.

Total _____

• Times I used the "say what you want" plan.

Total _____

SUPPLEMENTARY ACTIVITY #1

STP Spaghetti Message

This tangled-up piece of spaghetti has a message in it that will tell you a good STP plan for handling name-calling, put-downs, or situations in which someone is trying to make you mad. To find out what that message is, color in the circles that have a *. Then, follow along the spaghetti. Every time you come to a colored circle, write the letter in it on the line at the bottom of the page.

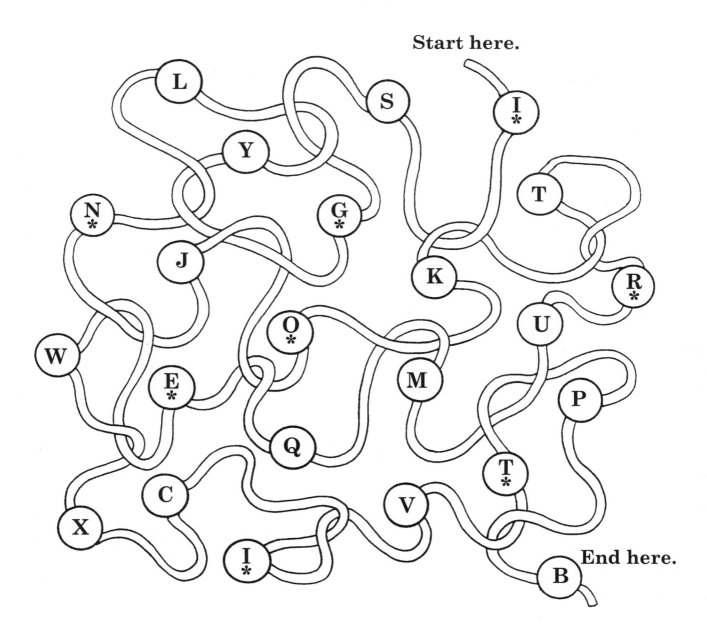

Start here.

End here.

When someone tries to make you mad:

__ __ __ __ __ __ __ __ __ __ __ __ __ __ __ __ __ __ __ __!

SUPPLEMENTARY ACTIVITY #2

More Practice With the "Ignore It" Plan

Objective   Students will demonstrate an ability to ignore provocative behavior in a calm, powerful manner.

Materials   Supplementary Activity #2 Teacher Sheets #1A and #1B, "'Ignore It!' Role-Play Cards" (cut cards apart and put them in a small box or basket)

Supplementary Activity #2 Transparency, "'Ignore It!' Role-Play Review"

Box or basket for cards

Procedure   Review the "ignore it" plan with your class. Demonstrate a noneffective way to ignore a situation (e.g., acting mad and stomping off or looking sad and hunched over) and an effective way to ignore a situation (e.g., calmly looking a person in the eyes and then walking away while standing up straight and tall).

Using Popsicle sticks, randomly choose ten students to pick an "Ignore It!" Role-Play Card. Have the student who draws Card #1 choose partners to work on the role-play with him or her. Then, in order, have the other nine students do the same thing. (Note the parentheses at the bottom of each card indicating the number of students required for the role-play. To accommodate variations in class size, some of the cards indicate a varying number. You can ensure that each student in your classroom is a part of a role-play group by writing in EXACT numbers in place of the varying numbers before the students select their cards. With some simple calculations you can easily make the total number of participants on the role-play cards match your class size.)

Once role-play groups are determined, have the students in each group work together to create an "ignore it" role-play based on the situation written on their card. After about 5 minutes invite the student groups to, one at a time, share their role-plays with the rest of the class, first reading the situation aloud and then acting it out. Have the Supplementary Activity transparency "'Ignore it!' Role-Play Review" on the overhead as the students are viewing the role-plays. While each group is acting out its role-play, instruct the rest of the class to watch for who used the "ignore it" plan, whether it was done in a calm but powerful way, and how ignoring the situation kept the problem from getting worse. Discuss each role-play at its conclusion. Highlight the calm, powerful way that students ignored various situations, as appropriate. Emphasize the power of the "ignore it" plan to keep a situation from getting worse.

"Ignore It!" Role-Play Cards

"Ignore It!" Role-Play Card #1

Your teacher tells the class to stay in their seats and work quietly on a project. She leaves the room. Some kids start throwing spitballs.

(4 or more students)

"Ignore It!" Role-Play Card #2

You're sitting at the back of the bus. Some kids around you start bouncing up and down in their seats, which is against bus rules.

(3 or more students)

"Ignore It!" Role-Play Card #3

You are talking with some of your friends. They begin to talk about one of your other friends, saying mean things.

(3 or more students)

"Ignore It!" Role-Play Card # 4

At recess a kid starts to bother you. She follows you around repeating everything you say.

(2 students)

"Ignore It!" Role-Play Card #5

You just got braces. You are walking down a street in your neighborhood and meet some kids. They start laughing at you.

(3 or more students)

"Ignore It!" Role-Play Card #6

You and a friend are playing a game. Your friend loses, gets really mad, and starts to use bad language.

(2 students)

"Ignore It!" Role-Play Cards (continued)

"Ignore It!" Role-Play Card #7 Your teacher asks you to answer a question for the class. You know the answer. The kid in back of you keeps kicking your chair. (2 students)	**"Ignore It!" Role-Play Card #8** You are taking a test. The kid sitting next to you asks in a whisper, "What's the answer to Number 5?" (2 students)
"Ignore It!" Role-Play Card #9 You and a friend are at the movies. Your friend starts talking to you right at a really exciting part of the movie. (2 students)	**"Ignore It!" Role-Play Card #10** You and a friend are at a baseball game. Your friend keeps bugging you to throw popcorn at the kids in the bleachers below you. (2 students)

SUPPLEMENTARY ACTIVITY #2 TRANSPARENCY

"Ignore It!" Role-Play Review

As each group does their role-play, watch for the answers to the following questions:

1. Who used the "ignore it" plan?

2. Was it done in a calm but powerful way?

3. How did ignoring the situation keep the problem from getting worse?

O.K. Ways to Tell Them to Stop

Objective   Students will select ways to tell someone to stop that they think will work well for them.

Materials   Supplementary Activity #3 Transparency/Handout, "O.K. Ways to Tell Them to Stop"

Transparency #5 from Lesson 4, "Tell Them to Stop"

Procedure   Give students Supplementary Activity #3 Handout, "O.K. Ways to Tell Them to Stop," and place the matching transparency on the overhead. Read through the handout with the students. Then have the students underline the two sentences that they like the best. Once the students have underlined their two favorite sentences, conduct a class vote on which two sentences are class favorites. To do so, read through the sentences again, having students raise their hand when you read a sentence that they have underlined. Jot down the tally of the number of raised hands next to each sentence on the transparency.

Following the class vote, show students Transparency #5 from Lesson 4, "Tell Them to Stop." Demonstrate how this technique can work with the two sentences that the class has chosen as favorites. Then invite volunteers to demonstrate the "tell them to stop" steps using one of the sentences they underlined on their handout.

SUPPLEMENTARY ACTIVITY #3 HANDOUT

O.K. Ways to Tell Them to Stop

The sentences below show different ways to tell people to stop doing something. After your teacher reads all of the sentences out loud, underline the two that you like the best.

Stop bugging me!

Stop trying to get attention.

That bothers me!

Don't do that!

You're not cool.

I've had it!

Leave me alone!

You can't make me angry.

Stop it!

Bug off!

Could you please quit it?

Cut it out!

Knock it off!

Your idea:

_____

_____

SUPPLEMENTARY ACTIVITY #4

STP Traffic Light

Make your own STP traffic light by coloring the three circles below. Color the "STOP" circle red. Color the "THINK" circle yellow. Color the "PLAN" circle green. Then cut out each circle and paste it in the appropriate place on the handout titled "My STP Traffic Light."

SUPPLEMENTARY ACTIVITY #4 HANDOUT

My STP Traffic Light

Whenever I feel like I want to fight,
I look at my STP traffic light.

Then I remember to STOP, THINK, and PICK A PLAN.
When it comes to making smart choices, I know I can!

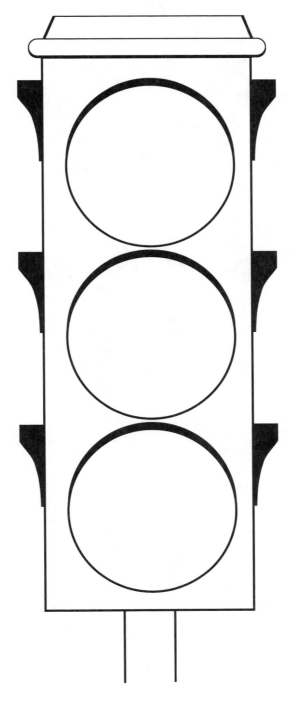

Lesson 5

<u>S</u>top, <u>T</u>hink, and Pick a <u>P</u>lan— A Conflict Resolution Process

STEP 3: Pick a <u>P</u>lan
Stay and Make a Deal (Negotiate)

Stop, Think, and Pick a Plan—
A Conflict Resolution Process

STEP 3: Pick a Plan
Stay and Make a Deal (Negotiate)

Objective   Students will learn the strategy of making a deal in a conflict situation.

Materials   Transparency #1 from Lesson 4 – "STP: Stop, Think, and Pick a Plan"

Transparency #6 from Lesson 4 – "On the Watch for the 'Ignore It' and the 'Say What You Want' Plans"

Transparency #2 from Lesson 4 – "The Pick a Plan Step (What to Do If You Stay)"

Transparency #1 – "How to Make a Deal (Negotiate)"

Transparency #2 – "Sharing"

Transparency #3/Handout #1 – "Things to Do While You're Waiting Your Turn"

Handout #2 – "I Can Make a Deal"

Scruffy the STP Dog puppet from Lesson 1

Poster – "Make a Deal"

To the Teacher

This lesson teaches the strategy that students will probably use the most when attempting to resolve a conflict, the strategy of making a deal, or negotiating. The assumption in this lesson is that the conflict involves (1) a scarcity of resources, such as supplies or play equipment; (2) time issues, such as time divided between different friends; or (3) power issues, such as who will be captain or classroom monitor. Students will learn three ways to negotiate or work out these types of conflicts: sharing, taking turns, and swapping (or trading).

In the discussion of sharing, it is important to acknowledge that sharing can sometimes be difficult and to talk about appropriate and inappropriate times to share. In the discussion of taking turns, students will learn some practical ways to enhance patience. The strategy of swapping is taught by encouraging the students to guess what another person would want or what would please the other person and how they could provide that. They will practice resolving situations by having both people in a conflict get part of what they want.

At the end of this lesson, we recommend that you display the poster that reinforces the lesson concept in a place where students will be able to use it as a reminder for the rest of the week.

Lesson Presentation

REVIEW OF PREVIOUS LESSONS

**Lesson 4, Transp. #1
Lesson 4, Transp. #6**

Show Transparency #1 from Lesson 4, "STP: Stop, Think, and Pick a Plan." Review the "stop," "think," and "pick a plan" steps, sliding a piece of paper down the page to uncover each step as you review it. When you get to the "pick a plan" step, cover up the "If you stay" column and remind the students that they know three things to do if they choose to walk away from a conflict: get help, do something else, and take time to cool down. Remind them that they also know two things to do if they decide to stay and work out a disagreement. Say: **I'd like each of you to turn to your learning partner and see who can be the first to say the two plans.** *After a few seconds have the kids who were first raise their thumbs. Accept ties. Then uncover the "If you stay" list on the transparency and say, pointing to the plans as you mention them,* **During this past week you were to keep track of times you or someone else used the "say what you want" or the "ignore it" plan.** *Show Transparency #6 from Lesson 4, "On the Watch for the 'Ignore It' and the 'Say What You Want' Plans" and ask the students to get out their handouts. Tell the students to total up their tally marks and place their totals on the lines at the right. Then have student volunteers report on their observations of others. Ask them which plan they observed people using more, the "ignore it" plan or the "say what you want" plan. Continue by discussing students' observations of their own behavior, again asking them which plan they used the most—ignoring or saying what they want. Ask the students to describe situations in which they observed or used one of the plans.*

INTRODUCE THE "MAKE A DEAL" PLAN

Lesson 4, Transp. #2

Following the review, say: **Today I'm going to show you another plan you can use if you are caught in a conflict.** *Show Transparency #2 from Lesson 4, "The Pick a Plan Step (What to Do If You <u>Stay</u>)."* **You already know what to do if you decide to walk away from a conflict, and it sounds like a lot of you know how to use the "ignore it" and "say what you want" plans when you decide to stay in a conflict and try to resolve it. As you can see here, there are three more plans that can help you if you decide to stay and work things out. You can "make a deal," "use chance," or "say you're sorry."**

Today we're going to talk about the "make a deal" plan. *Circle or underline "MAKE A DEAL" on the transparency.* **It's a great plan, and you'll probably discover that this is the plan you will use most often to work out disagreements or conflicts in your life. Last time we talked about the "say what you want" plan. That plan can work well when the other person doesn't realize what you really want and is willing to change what he or she is doing once you've said something. But sometimes the other person may want something different from what you want.**

For example, remember our discussion in the last lesson about a friend who comes to your house and takes a favorite toy off your shelf to play with. You don't want the friend to play with it, but your friend doesn't know that until you tell him or her what you want. You might say something like, "That's my favorite toy. I just got it and I don't want anyone to play with it. Please put it back." Your friend <u>might</u> say, "Oh! O.K. Sorry!" <u>But</u>, your friend might also really, really want to play with that toy. So, instead, your friend might say, "I'll be really careful with it. Come on, let me play with it!" If this happens, a good way to work out the problem might be to make an agreement or a deal with your friend.

Transp. #1

Show Transparency #1, "How to Make a Deal (Negotiate)." **Working out a problem and coming to an agreement with someone else is called negotiating.** *Point to the word "negotiate" on the transparency. Cover the rest of the transparency.* **When you negotiate, or make a deal,** you lose something but you get something, too. Let me give you an example to explain. Two friends want to play on the bars, but there's only one space left. They decide to make a deal and each use the bars for half of the recess. By doing this, each kid loses something—getting to spend the whole recess on the bars—but each kid gets something, too. They each get to spend half of the recess on the bars, and they get to keep their friendship. They also avoid getting into a big fight, which would ruin both of their recesses.

Making a deal can prevent a lot of trouble. It's not that hard to come up with a deal. By the end of this lesson, you'll have learned three ways that you can make a deal with someone you are having an argument with. *Uncover the rest of the transparency.* They are to share, to take turns, and to swap.

MAKE A DEAL BY SHARING

All of you know what it means to share. Who can give an example of how you could work out a problem with someone by sharing? *Allow for student response.*

Sharing can really help stop a little argument from turning into a big fight, but it's not always appropriate. Sharing works well with things that are easy to share, but it may not be the best plan when it involves things that are really tough to share.

Transp. #2

Show Transparency #2, "Sharing." Let's make a list of things you would find easy to share and things you would find hard to share. As we make the list, someone might suggest something that you think is hard to share for the list of things that are easy to share, or vice versa. That's O.K. Everyone is different. Some things will be easy for one person to share and hard for another. *Brainstorm items for the list with the class. Write the students' suggestions on the transparency under the headings "Things That Are Easy to Share" and "Things That Are Hard to Share."*

Point to the list of things that are hard to share. Say: **Things like a favorite toy can be really tough to share. In fact, you might have some special treasure that you won't ever choose to share because it's so important to you. In conflicts involving things like that you'd probably want to make a deal in another way—one that doesn't involve sharing—or find another plan to try.**

However, when a conflict revolves around something that is easy for you to share, you'll probably find that sharing is one of the best ways to work out the problem. For instance, pretend that a friend really wants the candy bar that your mom packed in your lunch. Your friend keeps begging for it. The candy bar is one of your favorites, but you know that there's another one you can have when you get home. You might work out the problem and come to an agreement by suggesting that you both share the candy bar.

How many of you think that making a sharing deal would be a good way to work out this problem? *Allow for student response. Note that even in this situation sharing might be comfortable for some kids but not for others.*

Continue by saying: **Let me give you one more example of a time when sharing might be a good way to work out a problem with another person. Pretend that you are doing an art project in class using clay. The teacher has given everyone the same amount of clay. You are making a bird's nest with eggs and your friend is making a log cabin. Just as you finish the nest, your friend says he needs some of your clay to finish his log cabin. You might decide to make one egg instead of five and to share most of your clay with him.**

How many of you think that making a sharing deal would be a good way to work out this problem? *Allow for student response. As before, it is important to recognize that even in this situation sharing might be comfortable for some kids but not for others.*

Summarize by saying: **Sharing is often a good way to handle problems involving two people wanting the same thing, such as food or classroom supplies like clay, glue, or construction paper. Sharing is especially effective when the two people are friends. When you have a conflict with someone and you share, you are making a deal. To make a deal, or "negotiate," means to work out a problem and come to an agreement together. One way you can make a deal is by sharing something.**

MAKE A DEAL BY TAKING TURNS

Transp. #1

Show Transparency #1, "How to Make a Deal (Negotiate)," once again. Say: **Taking turns is another great way to make a deal when two people want the same thing. Who can tell us about a time when deciding to take turns helped keep you from getting into a fight with someone?** *Allow for student response.*

**Transp. #3
Handout #1**

Taking turns will solve many conflicts, but sometimes it can be hard to wait your turn. It's often a good idea to set a specific length of time for each person's turn. That way, you'll know just how long you'll have to wait. It can also help to do something else while you're waiting so that the time doesn't seem so long until it's your turn. *Show Transparency #3, "Things to Do While You're Waiting Your Turn," and give students the handout of the same title. Read the list of ideas to the class. Have the students underline the ideas they might like to use the next time they decide to take turns and are waiting for their turn. Take a tally of which idea is a class favorite by having students raise their hands as you read the list a second time. Then ask the students:* **What are other things that you do to pass the time while you wait your turn?** *Write the students' suggestions on the overhead.*

When you have a conflict with another person and you take turns, you are making a deal. To make a deal, or "negotiate," means to work out a problem and come to an agreement together. One way you can make a deal is by sharing. Another way is by taking turns.

MAKE A DEAL BY SWAPPING

Transp. #1

Once again show Transparency #1, "How to Make a Deal (Negotiate)." **You all have probably used sharing and taking turns before to handle a problem with someone. Now I want to talk to you about another way to make a deal that you might not have used before.** *Point to the word "swap" on the transparency.* **When you have a disagreement with someone you may be able to work out the problem and come to an agreement by suggesting a swap. To make a deal by swapping something means to offer something the other person wants so that you can get something you want. Let me give you an example.**

Puppet

Ask for a volunteer to come up to the front of the class and work out a problem with Scruffy. Give a piece of red construction paper to the student and a piece of green construction paper to Scruffy. Explain to the class: **Scruffy and his friend** *(state the name of the student)* **are working on a Christmas project in their classroom. Both of them want to make a green Christmas tree with red decorations. Scruffy got the last piece of green paper.** *(Student's name)* **got the last piece of red paper. Let's listen in to see how they can make a deal that will solve their problem.**

Scruffy: **I'm <u>so</u> glad I got the green paper. I want to make a <u>big</u> Christmas tree that takes up the <u>whole</u> paper!**

Teacher: *(Prompting student) (Student's name),* **you need some green paper, too. And Scruffy wants some red paper. What could you suggest to Scruffy so that you can get some of his green paper? Remember, to make a deal by swapping, you offer something the other person wants so that you can get something you want.** *Allow time for the student to negotiate a swap with Scruffy.*

Scruffy: **Hum. I guess I could make my tree smaller than I wanted to. I <u>do</u> want some red paper to make decorations for the tree. How about if we get some scissors and cut both of our papers in half?** *Allow time for student response.*

Teacher: **Good job!** *(To class)* **Scruffy and** *(student's name)* **solved the problem of both wanting the same colors of paper without fighting. Instead, they made a deal. What did they decide to do?** *Allow for student response.* **You're right—they decided to "swap."** *(Name of student)* **offered Scruffy some of the red paper that Scruffy wanted in order to get some of the green paper that** *(he/she)* **wanted. Thank you, Scruffy and** *(name of student)* **for helping me show the class what it means to make a deal by swapping.**

Invite another student to come to the front of the room to do a swap role-play with Scruffy. Explain that the student and Scruffy are eating lunch together. Scruffy has a candy bar that is the student's favorite. The student can hardly stand to see it sitting in Scruffy's lunch box, let alone think about Scruffy eating it without sharing it with him or her. Instruct the student to ask Scruffy to share half of the candy bar with him or her.

Scruffy: **No. I really like this candy bar. Why should I share it with you?**

Teacher: *(Whispering in student's ear in a loud whisper so the class can hear)* **Scruffy also really likes homemade chocolate chip cookies. You have two in your lunch. What could you suggest to Scruffy?** *Allow time for the student to make a deal with Scruffy by suggesting a swap.*

Scruffy: **O.K., I'll give you half of my candy bar for both of your cookies.**

Teacher: **What do you think,** *(student's name)***? You** <u>**really**</u> **want that candy bar!** *Allow time for the student to respond to Scruffy.*

Continue by saying to the class: **When you want to make a deal by swapping you have to think about what the other person would want. Keep in mind that sometimes what the other person wants may be something really different from what you want. Scruffy told me about being in just that situation a short time ago. Scruffy's favorite thing is to take care of the classroom gerbil. The teacher had made out a schedule where everybody got a week**

to be in charge of the gerbil. Scruffy was absent for all but one day during the week that he was on gerbil duty. *Turn to Scruffy and say:* **Scruffy, tell the class what you did when you got to school the next week and saw that Sasha was on gerbil duty for the week.**

Scruffy: **Well, I asked Sasha if I could take over her duty.**

Teacher: **What did she say?**

Scruffy: **She said, "No way," that it was her week. And I even explained to her how I lost my turn because I'd been sick. She still said no and told me to stop bugging her.**

Teacher: **So what did you do, Scruffy?**

Scruffy: **Well, I thought to myself, "There's got to be a way I can get some time with that gerbil." So I started thinking about things I had that Sasha might like. Then I remembered my invisible ink marking pens! I decided to ask her if she wanted to make a deal. I said that she could keep my invisible ink marking pens in her desk and use them for the whole week if I could be on gerbil duty for half of her week.**

Teacher: **Did she take you up on your deal?**

Scruffy: **Yup. It worked!**

Turn to the class and say: **How many of you have ever made a deal with someone by offering something he or she wanted in order to get something that you wanted? Raise your hands.** *Allow for student response, letting several students discuss times when they swapped something.*

Swapping can be a good way to make a deal with someone when you can find something that each of you has that the other wants. Swapping can be fun, too. Instead of getting into a big fight with each other, you both give up something but you also get something. So, you both end up having something you wouldn't have had if you hadn't decided to swap.

Point to "Swap" on Transparency #1, "How to Make a Deal (Negotiate)." **When you have a conflict with another person and you swap, you are making a deal. To make a deal, or "negotiate," means to work out a problem and come to an agreement together. One way you can make a deal is by sharing. Another way is by taking turns. Still another way is by swapping.**

"MAKE A DEAL" PRACTICE

Let's have some fun with the three ways of making a deal that we have talked about today. I'm going to tell you about some situations that kids your age might face where making a deal could help keep a disagreement from turning into a big fight. After I've finished describing each situation, I want you to choose whether you would share, take turns, or swap to make a deal. If you would share in the situation, clap your hands twice. *Point to "Share" on Transparency #1, "How to Make a Deal (Negotiate)." Write "clap twice" next to it as a reminder.* **If you would take turns, stamp your feet twice.** *Write "stamp twice" next to "Take Turns" as a reminder.* **If you would swap in the situation, tap your desk with your hand twice.** *Write "tap desk twice" next to "Swap" as a reminder.*

Although some of the ways to make a deal will work better than others in different situations, there are no right or wrong choices for any situation. The important thing is to choose a way of making a deal that will help you work out a problem with somebody else by coming to an agreement together. Sometimes the best way to do that will be to share something that you have. Other times you can take turns. And other times you'll be able to give something <u>and</u> get something back by swapping.

Now, let's see what you'll decide to do in the situations I'm going to read. After you've voted on each, I'm going to use our Popsicle sticks to select several of you to tell me what way of making a deal you chose and why. *Read the following scenarios, cueing students after each one to vote and then calling on several students to tell what they would do and why.*

- Jill and Jesse both want to use a certain game during free time in class. They both reach for the game at the same time. They need to make a deal with each other. What kind of deal should they make?

- George and Hector both want to sit by Scruffy on the bus, but only two kids are allowed per seat. They need to make a deal. What kind of deal should they make?

- Five kids want to play follow the leader at recess, but they all want to be the leader. They need to make a deal. How do they decide who will be the leader?

- Silas wants to borrow Cliff's new Nintendo game. Silas owns a game that he knows Cliff really likes. What sort of deal could Silas make?

- Pauline and Molly are working on their art projects in class. Pauline runs out of glue before she finishes her project. She wants some of Molly's glue. Molly isn't sure she will have enough glue to finish her project if she gives some to Pauline. How could the girls make a deal to solve this problem?

- Jesse and Petra are friends. They have both been waiting together in line to use the parallel bars. Finally Jesse gets a place on the bars, but there is no room for Petra and the recess time is almost over. What should they do?

REVIEW AND HOMEWORK

Remove Transparency #1, "How to Make a Deal (Negotiate)," from the overhead. Say to the class: **I think you've got it! You now know several ways to make a deal. Who can say the three ways that you've learned to make a deal?** *Allow for student response, calling on several students to recite the three ways.*

Now I have a harder question for you. Who knows another way to say "make a deal"? It's one word and it begins with an "n." *Allow for student response.* **Yes, that's right. "Negotiate." It means to make a deal. When you negotiate, or make a deal, you work out a problem and come to an agreement together. It's a mouthful, but it's a word that you're going to be using a lot in your life because it's so much better to make a deal with someone than to fight.**

Handout #2

As I said at the beginning of this lesson, you'll probably discover that this is the plan you will use most often to work out disagreements or conflicts in your life. *Give students Handout #2, "I Can Make a Deal." Explain that for homework this week they should try to use each one of the ways to make a deal that they have learned. Then they should draw a picture of themselves using each of the different ways to make a deal. If they are not in a conflict situation in which they can make a deal during the week, they should draw themselves in an imagined situation.*

SUPPLEMENTARY ACTIVITIES

Use the supplementary activities that follow this lesson to reinforce the lesson concepts.

- *"Make a Deal" Mystery Puzzle*
  (Supplementary Activity #1)

- *"Scruffy Makes a Deal" Storybook*
  (Supplementary Activity #2)

- *Origami Scruffy*
  (Supplementary Activity #3)

- *Share and Take Turns*
  (Supplementary Activity #4)

- *Taking Turns*
  (Supplementary Activity #5)

- *Sharing*
  (Supplementary Activity #6)

TRANSPARENCY #1

How to Make a Deal
(Negotiate)

1. Share

2. Take Turns

3. Swap

TRANSPARENCY #2

Sharing

<u>Things That Are Easy to Share:</u>

<u>Things That Are Hard to Share:</u>

TRANSPARENCY #3/HANDOUT #1

Things to Do
While You're Waiting Your Turn

1. Do some other activity while you're waiting, such as playing with a different toy or jumping rope.

2. Think about something interesting that gets your mind off the thing you're waiting for.

3. Read or draw to make the time go faster.

4. Make up a story for a TV show or movie in your head.

5. Enjoy watching the other person do the activity.

6. Play with your pet.

Your ideas:

_____

_____

_____

_____

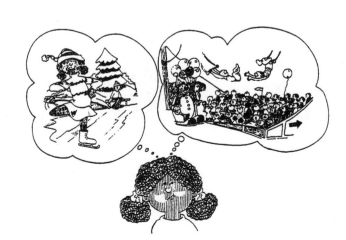

HANDOUT #2

I Can Make a Deal

In each box below, draw yourself solving a real or imagined conflict with someone by making a deal in one of the three ways you have learned.

SHARE

TAKE TURNS

SWAP

POSTER

Make a Deal

Share, Take Turns, or Swap

SUPPLEMENTARY ACTIVITY #1

I was here first!

You lost your place!

"Make a Deal" Mystery Puzzle

These two kids are having an argument. They need to make a deal. What kind of deal could they make? To find out, use a green crayon or marker and shade in all the spaces that contain the letter "D."

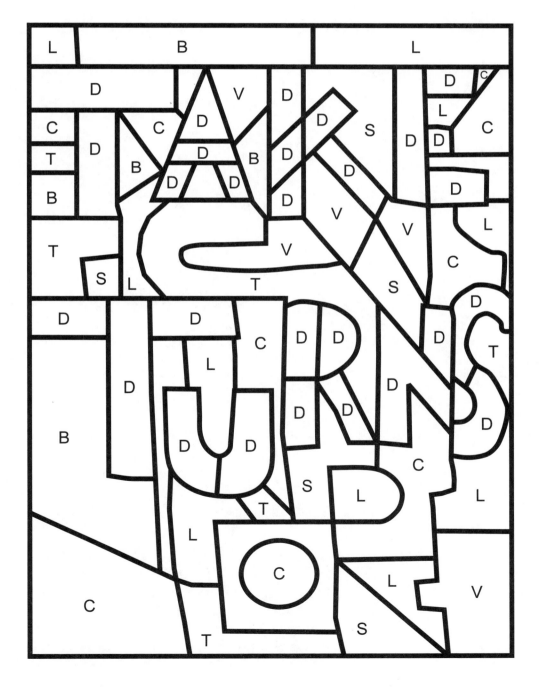

SUPPLEMENTARY ACTIVITY #2

"Scruffy Makes a Deal" Storybook

Cut out the picture of Scruffy on the "Scruffy Pattern" handout and trace it onto two pieces of construction paper. Then cut out the Scruffy shapes. These will be the front and back covers for your storybook. Next, trace the picture onto several sheets of lined paper and cut out the Scruffy shapes. These will be the pages for your storybook.

Make up a story about a time when Scruffy had a problem with someone and needed to make a deal. Then write a story about Scruffy using sharing, taking turns, or swapping to solve the problem.

Once you have written your story, put the pages in between the front and back covers and staple them all together on the side or the top. Share your story with other members of your class.

SUPPLEMENTARY ACTIVITY #2 HANDOUT

Scruffy Pattern

SUPPLEMENTARY ACTIVITY #3 HANDOUT #1

Origami Scruffy

Follow the diagrams on this page (Handout #1) and the next page (Handout #2) to make an origami Scruffy. When you have finished, place your Scruffy on the corner of your desk or take it home and put it somewhere in your bedroom to remind you to use STP when you get into a conflict with someone.

HEAD

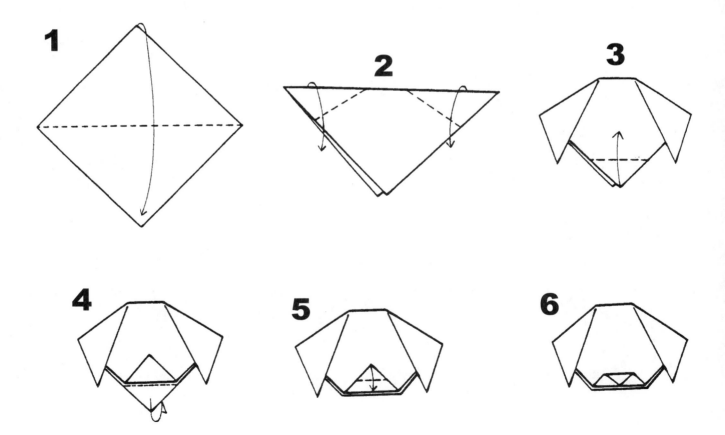

Origami Scruffy (continued)

BODY

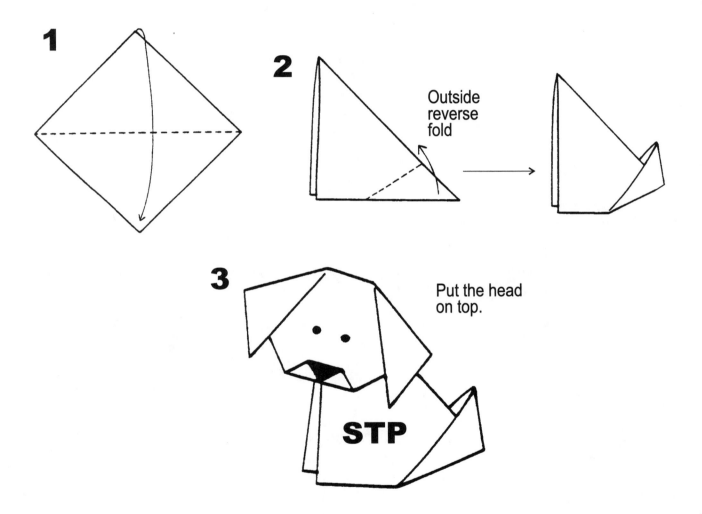

1

2 Outside reverse fold

3 Put the head on top.

STP

Then, color Scruffy's nose,

give Scruffy eyes, and

write "STP" on Scruffy's body.

SUPPLEMENTARY ACTIVITY #4

Share and Take Turns

Objective   Students will raise their awareness about their own ability to share and take turns and will set a goal concerning one of these behaviors.

Materials   Supplementary Activity #4 Handout, "Share and Take Turns"

Procedure   Give students Supplementary Activity #4 Handout, "Share and Take Turns," and say that you will read each item to them. Explain that they should ask themselves, for each item, whether they do the behavior "sometimes," "always," or "never" and should then put a check in the appropriate box. Explain that you won't be looking at their responses. Tell them that the purpose of this activity is to help them increase their own awareness of how much they share and take turns, so they can be honest in their answers without fear of embarrassment. They should **ask themselves** each question after you read it and simply "wait for their brain to give them the answer."

After the students have completed the questionnaire, they should pick one behavior that they would like to improve. It doesn't have to be the behavior they do the least often. It could even be the behavior that they do the most often but think they could improve upon. They should pick a behavior that wouldn't be too hard for them to change and that would make them like themselves better if they improved it. They should write their goal in the space provided at the bottom of the handout.

Explain that a wise man named William James discovered that the easiest way to get rid of a bad behavior and replace it with a better one is to do the following two things:

1.   Start immediately.

2.   Tell others what you're going to do.

Tell the students that they should therefore start working on the behavior this very day and that you would like each of them to share with the class the behavior they've picked.

Quickly go around the class having each student share his or her "goal." Students might want to cut out their goal statement and tape it to the inside of their STP folder to provide themselves with a reminder. Over the next few days, remind the students to implement their goals when opportunities arise.

SUPPLEMENTARY ACTIVITY #4 HANDOUT

Share and Take Turns

Sharing and taking turns are two ways to prevent fights and solve problems. Ask yourself these questions and see what answer your brain gives back.

How willing are you to share?	Sometimes	Always	Never
1. I ask other kids to join in my games.			
2. I share play equipment at recess.			
3. I offer to share with a friend if I have a snack or a treat.			
4. I share my friends by letting them play with someone else.			

How willing are you to take turns?	Sometimes	Always	Never
1. I pass the ball during games.			
2. I take turns listening so other people can talk.			
3. I take turns by raising my hand before I talk.			
4. I don't take too long on the play equipment if someone else is waiting.			
5. I wait in line until it's my turn instead of pushing or crowding.			

One thing I will work on starting today is:

SUPPLEMENTARY ACTIVITY #5

Taking Turns

On the lines below, give some examples of times when ***taking turns*** could keep a small disagreement from turning into a big fight.

_____

_____

_____

_____

_____

Sharing

Complete the following sentence stems.

I don't mind sharing . . . _____

I do not like sharing . . . _____

I felt proud of myself when I shared . . . _____

Lesson 6

**<u>S</u>top, <u>T</u>hink, and Pick a <u>P</u>lan—
A Conflict Resolution Process**

STEP 3: Pick a <u>P</u>lan
Stay and Use Chance
or Say You're Sorry

<u>S</u>top, <u>T</u>hink, and Pick a <u>P</u>lan—
A Conflict Resolution Process

STEP 3: Pick a <u>P</u>lan
Stay and Use Chance or Say You're Sorry

Objective   Students will learn the strategies of "using chance" and "saying you're sorry" to resolve a conflict situation.

Materials   Transparency #2 from Lesson 4 – "The Pick a <u>P</u>lan Step (What to Do If You <u>Stay</u>)"

Transparency #1 – "Use Chance to Decide"

Teacher Sheets #1A, #1B, and #1C – "Chance Activities Sheet"

Transparency #2 – "Wheel of Chance"

Transparency #3 – "Sometimes It's Hard to Say You're Sorry"

Transparency #4 – "The 'Say You're Sorry' Plan"

Transparency #5 – "Saying You're Sorry Is a Gift You Give Someone"

Handout #1 – "Kids Can Use Chance Instead of Fighting"

Handout #2 – "A Time I Said 'I'm Sorry' and Meant It"

Poster #1 – "Use Chance—It's Quick and Fair"

Poster #2 – "Use Chance"

Poster #3 – "Say You're Sorry"

Scruffy the STP Dog puppet from Lesson 1

To the Teacher

In this lesson students will learn two final strategies that can help them if they decide to stay to work out a conflict: using chance and apologizing. Once they've mastered these skills, they will have a well-rounded repertoire of conflict resolution skills.

Chance is presented as a strategy that is easy, quick, and fair. Chance is an effective tool for passive students who tend to give in to others rather than expend the emotional energy required of some of the other conflict resolution plans such as negotiation.

Most of your students probably already know some techniques for using chance to decide an outcome. In the lesson, a number of well-known "chance" activities, including rhymes, guessing games, and activities that use objects or coordination will be discussed, and students will be asked to share any other activities they use with the class. In addition, they will learn a new rhyme entitled "Let Chance Decide It."

Although primary students have varying ability to empathize, it is important to encourage them to apologize if they feel responsible for hurting someone or if they're sorry that an incident occurred, even when they might not feel totally responsible for the incident. Students need to understand that saying they're sorry doesn't necessarily mean that they're wrong but rather that they care about how another person feels. In this lesson, the puppet Scruff is used to demonstrate the differences between hollow and heartfelt apologies. Students are cautioned about using apologies in a flippant or manipulative way.

At the end of this lesson, we recommend that you display the posters that reinforce the lesson concepts in a place where students will be able to use them as a reminder for the rest of the week.

Lesson Presentation

REVIEW OF PREVIOUS LESSONS

We've been practicing plans that you can use when you decide to stay and try to resolve an argument. Can anybody give me an example of one of the plans we've talked about? *Allow for student response. Show Transparency #2 from Lesson 4, "The Pick a Plan Step (What to Do If You Stay)," covering "use chance" and "say you're sorry" with Post-it notes. Tell the students that you are going to ask them some questions about the plans and will point to the plans on the overhead. As you do so, they should say the name of the plan as loud as they can. Begin with this question:* **What's something you can do when someone's bugging you?** *Point to the words "ignore it" on the overhead. Ask:* **What's something else you can do when someone's bugging you?** *Point to the words "say what you want" on the overhead.* **What's something you can do when you and somebody else both want the same thing at the same time?** *Point to the words "make a deal" on the overhead.* **Great! Now, can anyone remember three ways to make a deal?** *Allow for student response. Then ask the students to get their homework assignment from the last lesson out of their STP folders. Say:* **Hold your "I Can Make**

a Deal" handouts up in the air so we can all see the pictures of you using the three different ways of making a deal. Would anyone like to tell us about a time this week when you had a chance to use one of the ways to make a deal? *Allow for student response.*

Say: **Today we're going to talk about the last two STP plans: "use chance" and "say you're sorry."** *Remove the Post-it notes to reveal these plans on the overhead.*

"USE CHANCE" PLAN

Let's start with chance, because it can be a really quick and easy way to settle an argument. If you tend to give in to others who are bossier or older than you, you're going to like this plan. Instead of having to stand up for and demand what's fair, you can just say, "Let's let chance decide." Then the other person can blame chance instead of you if the outcome isn't what he or she wanted.

Using chance can be really fun, too, as long as both people agree to let luck decide and are good sports about how things turn out. For instance, let's say that you and another kid disagree over whether the ball was out of bounds. You both feel <u>sure</u> you're right, and neither one of you feels like giving in to the other. Why not let chance decide? That way, the two of you won't end up in a fight and you'll be able to quickly get on with the game.

Chance is also a good way to solve a disagreement that involves more than two people. For instance, let's say that a bunch of kids want to play soccer and they need to choose team captains. Most of the kids want to be captains. A quick way to decide who the captains will be is to use chance.

Transp. #1

There are a lot of different ways to use chance to decide an outcome. *Show Transparency #1, "Use Chance to Decide."* **You can do hand games like Rock, Paper, Scissors or Bear, Salmon, Mosquito. You can use rhymes like "Bubble Gum, Bubble Gum," "One Potato, Two Potato," or "Eeny, Meeny, Miney, Moe." You can use guessing games like guessing which hand something is in or**

guessing a number someone is thinking of. You can use coordination activities, like seeing who can balance longest on one foot or who can toss a stone into a circle. And if you've got dice, cards, straws, a coin, or a rock, you can use them to decide an outcome.

Let's see how many of these <u>you already know</u>. As I read through the list on the transparency, raise your hand if you know how to use the activity to decide who wins when there's an argument over something. *Read through the list and write down tallies in the appropriate column on the transparency. Review the chance ideas the students don't know using Teacher Sheets #1A, #1B, and #1C.*

I see that a lot of you already know quite a few ways to use chance to solve an argument. Does anyone know any other tricks that are not mentioned on this list? What about other rhymes that you use? *Allow for student response. Write down the tricks that are not on the list and do a tally of how many in the class know them.*

Let's see which chance activities are <u>your favorites</u>. I'm going to ask you to vote for your favorite two out of all of these. Think about which two activities are your favorites. Then, as I go through the list, raise one finger when I read one of them and then raise a second finger when I come to the other one. Once you have two fingers up, put your hand in your lap so that you remember to not vote again. *Go through the list and tally the votes for each strategy. Then point to the activities that have gotten the top three votes and ask for each:* **Can someone who voted for this activity tell me why you like it or some times it has worked for you?** *Allow for student response.*

Teacher Sheets #1A, #1B, and #1C

I think it's always fun to learn a new way to use chance to decide an argument. I'd like to teach you some new chance activities. *Teach students "Let Chance Decide It" from Teacher Sheet #1B, "Chance Activities Sheet," helping students to memorize the rhyme and then allowing them time to practice the rhyme with a partner or small group. In addition, make sure that all students know the game Rock It Out (see Teacher Sheet #1A). If they don't, group students who know the activity with students who don't and practice it.*

Transp. #2

Show students Transparency #2, "Wheel of Chance." Say: **Let's play a game with this Wheel of Chance.** *Draw a down-pointing arrow on the top edge of the overhead screen. Explain to the students:* **I'm going to spin the wheel. When it stops, the arrow will be pointing to one of the ideas. I'll then draw one of your names from the Popsicle stick can. Your job will be to make up and tell us a short story about some kids who were smart enough to use this chance idea instead of fighting.**

Play the game for a predetermined amount of time. Then say: **Now let's make a list of times when the smart thing to do would be to use one of these chance tricks instead of continuing to argue.** *Let the students know that you'll be calling on volunteers but you'll also be drawing some names from the Popsicle stick container, so everyone should be ready with an example. Write the example on a blank transparency.*

Summarize by saying: **The next time that you and other kids are in a dispute or an argument over something, think about whether one of the chance activities we talked about today would help solve the dispute. Also, if you see some younger kids on the playground arguing over who's going to be first or something like that, you might suggest in a nice way that they try something like Rock It Out, "Let Chance Decide It," or one of the other tricks.** *During the week reinforce this lesson concept by modeling the use of chance to resolve conflicts whenever it's appropriate by saying something like, "Hey guys, why don't you Rock It Out?"*

"SAY YOU'RE SORRY" PLAN

Lesson 4, Transp. #2

Show Transparency #2 from Lesson 4, "The Pick a Plan Step (What to Do If you Stay)," again and point to the "say you're sorry" plan. **Let's talk now about one last plan you can use to work out a problem with someone before it turns into a big fight. You can say you're sorry. An honest apology when you make a mistake can quickly solve problems you are having with someone and could even save a friendship. Saying you're sorry doesn't mean that the problem is all your fault. It doesn't mean that you're bad or wrong. Saying you're sorry just means <u>you're sorry about what happened</u>.**

Let's say that your foot is out in the aisle. A kid in your class walks by and trips over your foot, dropping the open can of paint he was carrying. The kid's really mad at you even though you didn't mean to trip him. Should you say you're sorry even though you didn't trip him on purpose? *Allow for student discussion. Then say:* **Saying you're sorry doesn't have to mean that you did something on purpose. It just means you feel bad that the whole thing happened. In situations in which you slip up and do something mean on purpose, saying you're sorry means you have the courage to do the right thing: admit that you were wrong.**

Transp. #3

Show Transparency #3, "Sometimes It's Hard to Say You're Sorry," using a small piece of paper or a Post-it note to cover up what is written in the bubble. Say: **Apologizing takes courage. This boy's trying to get up the courage to give an apology to a kid in his neighborhood. But he dreads doing it. What are some of the things he might be thinking?** *Allow for student response. If the students don't mention the following, you might suggest: "He'll probably act like it's all my fault if I say I'm sorry," "If I say I'm sorry, he'll think he can boss me around," and "He might dump me as a friend." Following the discussion, say:* **You're right. He may be thinking any of those things. But do you know what he <u>should</u> be thinking or saying to himself instead? He should be thinking, "Saying I'm sorry means I have courage."** *Uncover the words in the bubble.*

Saying you're sorry is also a sure sign that you're getting more mature. Have you ever heard a spoiled brat apologize? *Elicit responses from students, drawing out the naturally selfish nature of babies and immature children.*

When kids get older and more mature, they start thinking about other people's feelings instead of just their own. When they make a mistake, they're able to say, "I made a mistake; I'm sorry about it." It's not easy to do, but kids get better at it as they mature. Ask yourself if you're mature enough to admit it when you're wrong. *Pause.*

**Transp. #4
Puppet**

Let me show you three easy ways to make an apology. *Show Transparency #4, "The 'Say You're Sorry' Plan." Cover all but the first part.* **After you've decided it would be a good thing to say you're sorry, say the words in a voice that shows you mean it. Usually other kids can tell if you don't mean it. Kids have an amazing ability to spot a liar. Let Scruff and I show you what I mean.** *Turn to Scruff and say:* **Scruff. Would you help me do a little demonstration?**

Scruff: **Sure!**

Teacher: **O.K. I'm going to whisper in your ear what I want you to do.** *Make whispering noises.* **Ready, Scruff?**

Scruff: **Ready!**

Teacher: **Scruff, when you borrowed my Walkman you said you'd bring it back yesterday, and you still haven't brought it back. I was planning to use it today, Scruff!**

Scruff: *(In a flippant, offhand voice)* **Sorry!**

Teacher: *(To the class)* **Now we're going to run through the role-play again.** *(To Scruff)* **Scruff, when you borrowed my Walkman you said you'd bring it back yesterday, and you still haven't brought it back. I was planning to use it today, Scruff!**

Scruff: *(In a sincere voice)* **I'm sorry.**

Ask the class: **Which apology do you think Scruff really meant, the first one or the second one?** *Allow for student response.* **Have any of you ever gotten an apology that you didn't feel the person meant? Just raise your hands if that's happened to you. You don't need to say who did it. Now look around the class. It's clear that kids can tell a fake apology! It's better to not say anything if you're really not sorry.**

If you did something that bugged or hurt somebody but it was an accident, it's O.K. to add "I didn't mean to" or "I didn't do it on

purpose" after you say you're sorry. Don't make up any phony excuses, though. That just makes kids mad.

Uncover the middle part of the transparency. **Another way to say you're sorry is to tell the person you'll try to make up for happened. If you broke or lost something, you might offer to fix it or replace it; if you took more than your share, offer to give the person something else. Offer to do whatever it takes to make things right or fair.**

Uncover the bottom part of the transparency. **The best apologies of all are ones where the person says, "I'm sorry, and it won't happen again."**

Now I'm going to tell you about some things that have happened to Scruff that really hurt his feelings. These are times when Scruff really deserved an apology. As I read them, raise your hand if you'd like to come up and role-play the kid apologizing to Scruff. *After each role-play, have Scruff indicate whether the apology felt honest and made him feel better. If a student doesn't add "It won't happen again" to his or her apology when saying that would be appropriate, have Scruff say something like, "Well, I'd feel a lot better if he (she) said he (she) wouldn't do it again."*

Read the following scenarios to the students. Leave Transparency #4 on the overhead so that the students can use it as a reminder during the role-plays.

- **Scruff's friend told him he couldn't come over and play because his mom said he had to do his homework. Later Scruff found out that he had invited someone else over.**

- **Scruff was really proud of the model plane he had just built. He left it on his porch when his mom called him in to eat dinner. While he was in the house the kid next door came over, saw the plane, and started playing with it. He was zooming it through the air when he bumped one of the wings and it fell off. When Scruff saw what happened he felt terrible. He was mad and sad at the same time.**

- **Scruff found out from some kids that a friend had said something mean about him behind his back. When he saw his friend again he asked his friend why he said that.**

- When Scruff went up to bat, a kid on his team said, "Well, get ready to watch a strikeout." When he saw that Scruff heard him, he said to Scruff, "Just kidding!" Later, he and Scruff were riding home in the same carpool and Scruff was really mad.

Transp. #5

Show Transparency #5, "Saying You're Sorry Is a Gift You Give Someone." Saying you're sorry is kind of like giving a gift to someone. It doesn't mean that you're weak or bad. It means you have the courage to admit when you do things that upset someone else. It means you want to make it up to that person so that both of you will feel all right again.

PRACTICE WITH USING CHANCE AND SAYING YOU'RE SORRY

Let's play a game where you decide whether using chance or saying you're sorry is the better plan for solving a conflict. I'm going to divide the room right down the middle. Those of you on the window side are going to be the "Use Chance" kids. Those on the other side are going to be the "Say You're Sorry" kids.

I'm going to read some situations out loud. If you think the better plan is to use "chance" and you're on the chance side of the room, stand up. If you think the better plan is to apologize and you're on the "say you're sorry" side of the room, then you stand up. Here's how you can win points for your team. Say that the better plan is to use chance. I'll be calling on someone who has stood up to say a good chance technique. If you can do this within five seconds, you'll win five points for your team. And say that the best plan is to apologize. If I call on you and you can say at least two ways to apologize, you'll win five points for your team. Any questions? **O.K., here we go!** *Read the following scenarios, one at a time. Keep a tally of the points on the board or overhead.*

- At the lunch table you lose it and you smash your friend's dessert with your fork.

- You and your friend both want to be first to use the Sony PlayStation.

- **A person pushes you when you're in line and you step on the foot of the person behind you.**

- **You borrowed a classmate's green marker and lost it. She's really mad.**

- **You and your friend both want to play on the bars and there's only one spot open. You push your friend out of the way and run so fast that you get there first.** *(Saying you're sorry and using chance would both be appropriate here, so choose someone from each side of the room to say the plan.)*

- **You and another kid are in an argument about whether you were out or safe at second base.**

- **When your friend got his spelling paper back, you saw that he got a lot of words wrong. You yelled out, "You missed that many!?" Your friend refuses to speak to you.**

- **Your teacher says that one person at your table can be a buddy to the new student. Everybody at your table wants to be the new student's buddy.**

- **You're at your friend's house and you both want to be first when you're playing a game.**

REVIEW AND HOMEWORK

Lesson 4,
Transp. #2
Handout #1
Handout #2

Show Transparency #2 from Lesson 4, "The Pick a Plan Step (What to Do If You Stay)." Say: **Today we've learned about the last two choices in the "pick a plan" step: "use chance" and "say you're sorry." You've done a good job at practicing both of these. Does anyone know why we've bothered to learn about and practice these and the other plans?** *Allow for student response.* **Right! So that you'll use them and make our class and school a more peaceful place to be. Also, friendships are really important, and it's such a waste to let little arguments ruin a friendship. I hope that this week you'll practice using chance and saying you're sorry whenever it's the smart thing to do.** *Give students Handout #1, "Kids Can Use Chance Instead of Fighting," and Handout #2, "A Time I Said 'I'm Sorry' and Meant It," for homework. These can be copied back-to-back.*

SUPPLEMENTARY ACTIVITIES

Use the supplementary activities that follow this lesson to reinforce the lesson concepts.

- *Using the Eight STP Keys to Handle Conflicts
   (Supplementary Activity #1)*

- *Is Chance Fair?
   (Supplementary Activity #2)*

- *Bear, Salmon, Mosquito Game
   (Supplementary Activity #3)*

- *An "I'm Sorry" Note
   (Supplementary Activity #4)*

- *The STP Game (Phase 3)
   (Supplementary Activity #5)*

- *STP Your Way to School Game
   (Supplementary Activity #6)*

- *Using Chance
   (Supplementary Activity #7)*

TRANSPARENCY #1

Use Chance to Decide

1. **Hand Games:**

   _____ _____   * Rock It Out (Rock, Paper, Scissors)

   _____ _____   * Bear, Salmon, Mosquito

2. **Rhymes:**

   _____ _____   * "Bubble Gum, Bubble Gum"

   _____ _____   * "One Potato, Two Potato"

   _____ _____   * "Eeny, Meeny, Miney, Moe"

   _____ _____   * "Engine, Engine, Number 9"

   _____ _____   * "A, B, C, D"

3. **Guessing Games:**

   _____ _____   * Guess which hand

   _____ _____   * Guess a number

4. **Use Coordination:**

   _____ _____   * Balance on one foot

   _____ _____   * Toss a stone into a circle

5. **Use Things:**

   _____ _____   * Draw straws, sticks, paper strips, or grass

   _____ _____   * High card

   _____ _____   * Throw dice

   _____ _____   * Flip a coin or a rock

TEACHER SHEET #1A

Chance Activities Sheet

Hand Games

Rock It Out, or Rock, Paper, Scissors

This is an activity for handling a conflict between two people. Each person faces the other and chants "Rock, Paper, Scissors" while beating the rhythm with a fist in the palm of one hand. When they come to the word "Scissors" each person makes a hand sign of one of the three symbols. The hand signs for rock, paper, and scissors are illustrated at right. Winning signs are as follows:

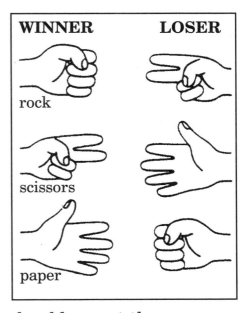

- Paper covers Rock, so Paper wins.
- Stone breaks Scissors, so Stone wins.
- Scissors cut Paper, so Scissors wins.

Note: If both people make the same sign they should repeat the game.

Bear, Salmon, Mosquito

This is another activity for handling a conflict between two people. Each person faces the other and chants "Bear, Salmon, Mosquito" while beating the rhythm with a fist in the palm of one hand. When they come to the word "Mosquito" each person makes a hand sign of one of the three symbols. The hand signs for bear, salmon, mosquito are:

bear
(a claw shape)

salmon
(two hands with palms
pressed together)

mosquito
(represents a stinger)

Winning signs are as follows:
- Bear eats Salmon, so Bear wins.
- Salmon eats Mosquito, so Salmon wins.
- Mosquito (carrying malaria) bites Bear, so Mosquito wins.

Note: If both people make the same sign they should repeat the game.

TEACHER SHEET #1B

Chance Activities Sheet (continued)

Rhymes

The following rhymes can be used to settle a dispute between two or more people. The people involved in the dispute may form a circle, each putting a fist (or foot) into the circle. A caller starts around the circle tapping each fist (or foot) and chanting the rhyme. When the rhyme ends, that person who is being tapped is the winner.

"Let Chance Decide It"
You first, me first. How will we know who's right?
Let chance decide it. And we won't have a fight.
(Person chooses "YES," "NO," or "MAYBE SO.")
Y-E-S spells yes./N-O spells no./M-A-Y-B-E S-O spells maybe so.

"Bubble Gum, Bubble Bum"
Bubble gum, bubble gum, in a dish.
How many pieces do you wish?
(Person says a number between 1 and 10.
The caller taps it out around the circle.)

"One Potato, Two Potato"
One potato, two potatoes, three potatoes, four.
Five potatoes, six potatoes, seven potatoes, more.

"Eeny, Meeny, Miney, Moe"
Eeny, Meeny, Miney, Moe;
Catch a monkey by his toe.
If he hollers, make him pay;
Fifty dollars every day!
My mother told me to pick the very best one and you are it!

"Engine, Engine, Number 9"
Engine, Engine, Number 9,
Going down Chicago line.
If the train should jump the track,
Do you want your money back?
(Person chooses "YES," "NO," or "MAYBE SO.")
Y-E-S spells yes./N-O spells no./M-A-Y-B-E S-O spells maybe so.

"A, B, C, D"
A, b, c, d, e, f, g, h, i, j, k, l,
m, n, o, p, q, r, s, t, U are it!

TEACHER SHEET #1c

Chance Activities Sheet (continued)

Guessing Games: Used to settle a dispute between two people.

Guess Which Hand

One kid holds something small in one hand. The other kid tries to guess which hand the object is in. If he or she guesses correctly, he or she wins. If he or she guesses incorrectly, the other kid wins.

Guess a Number

Have a third person think of a number between 1 and 10 and write it down. The two kids guess, and the one who guesses closest to the actual number wins.

Use Coordination: Used to settle a dispute between two or more people.

Balance on One Foot

One kid holds something small in one hand. The other kid tries to guess which hand the object is in. If he or she guesses correctly, he or she wins. If he or she guesses incorrectly, the other kid wins.

Toss a Stone Into a Circle

Students draw a small circle on the ground. Each of them picks a stone up and tries to toss it into the circle. The one closest to getting his or her stone into the circle wins.

Use Things: The first three activities are used to settle a dispute between two or more people. The fourth is used to settle a dispute between two people.

Draw Straws, Sticks, Paper Strips, or Grass

One student who is not involved in the dispute holds a number of straws, sticks, strips of paper, or grass cut into different lengths. All of the other students draw one straw, stick, etc. The student who draws the longest one wins.

High Card

Students draw a card from a deck of cards. The student who draws the highest card is the winner. (The students need to decide beforehand whether aces are "high" or "low.")

Throw Dice

Students, in turn, toss dice. The student who rolls the highest number wins.

Flip a Coin or a Rock

Two students call which side of the coin or rock they want (e.g., heads or tails, rough side or smooth side, marked side or unmarked side). The coin or rock is flipped in the air. The person who called the side that lands faceup is the winner.

TRANSPARENCY #2

Wheel of Chance

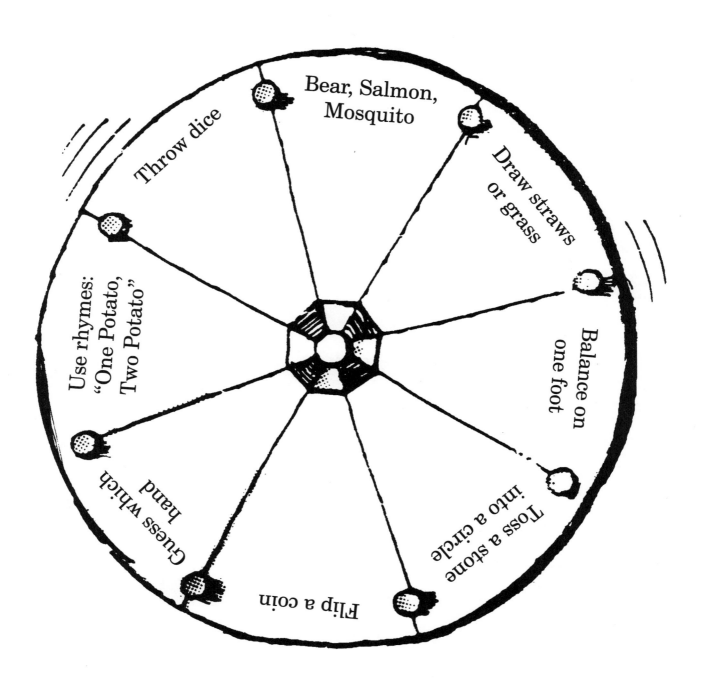

TRANSPARENCY #3

Sometimes It's Hard to Say You're Sorry

TRANSPARENCY #4

The "Say You're Sorry" Plan

· **Say you're sorry in a voice that sounds like you mean it.**

I'm sorry.

· **Try to make up for what happened.**

I'm sorry.
I'll help you fix it.

· **Say it won't happen again.**

I'm sorry, and
it won't happen again.

TRANSPARENCY #5

Saying You're Sorry Is a Gift You Give Someone

HANDOUT #1

Kids Can Use Chance Instead of Fighting

Show the Chance Wheel, below, to someone who takes care of you. Explain as many of these chance tricks to that person as you can. Have the person put a star after each one you're able to explain. Tell the person some times when it would be good to use these tricks.

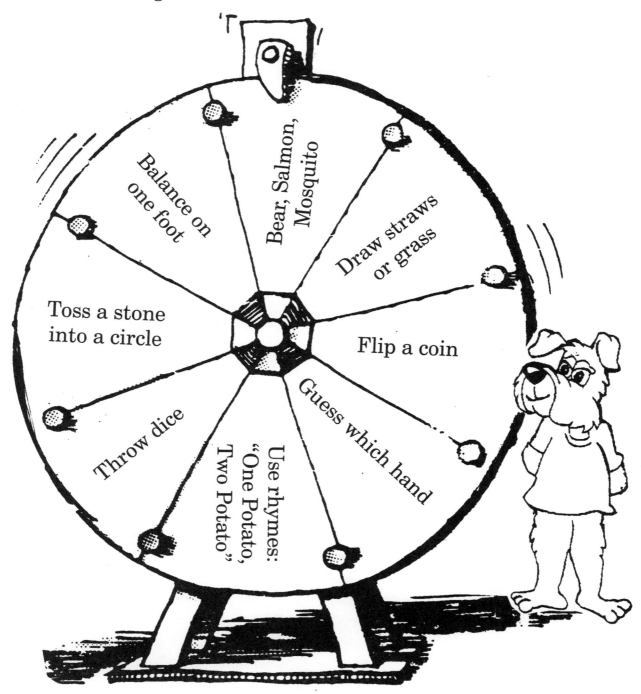

HANDOUT #2

A Time I Said "I'm Sorry" and Meant It

I'm sorry I was so crabby!

1. In the left-hand box draw yourself doing something that upset someone or hurt his or her feelings.
2. In the right-hand box draw yourself saying "I'm sorry" to the person.

| | |
| | |

Draw what happened   **Draw yourself saying you're sorry**

POSTER #1

Use Chance

It's Quick and Fair

1. **Hand Games:**
   * Rock It Out (Rock, Paper, Scissors)
   * Bear, Salmon, Mosquito

2. **Rhymes:**
   * "Let Chance Decide It"
   * "Bubble Gum, Bubble Gum"
   * "One Potato, Two Potato"
   * "Eeny, Meeny, Miney, Moe"
   * "Engine, Engine, Number 9"
   * "A, B, C, D"

3. **Guessing Games:**
   * Guess which hand
   * Guess a number

4. **Use Coordination:**
   * Balance on one foot
   * Toss a stone into a circle

5. **Use Things:**
   * Draw straws, sticks, paper strips, or grass
   * High card
   * Throw dice
   * Flip a coin or a rock

POSTER #2

Use Chance

POSTER #3

Say You're Sorry

Using the Eight STP Keys to Handle Conflicts

Objective   Students will practice working with the STP key plans for handling conflicts.

Materials   Supplementary Activity #1 Handouts #1A and #1B, "My STP Keys for Handling Conflicts" (copied onto stiff paper)

String or yarn, key rings or paper clips, scissors, colored markers, hole punch

Procedure   Give students a copy of both handouts. Have them color each key lightly, so that they can still read the words. Then have them cut out the keys and punch a hole where indicated on the keys. The students should then connect the keys using a string, piece of yarn, key ring, or paper clip.

Explain to the students that at the beginning of each day for the next eight school days you will write a number from 1 to 8 on the chalkboard. The students will then look through their ring of keys and find the key that has that number written on it. They will arrange their ring of keys so that this key is visible and set the key ring on the corner of their desk. For the rest of the day, the students should focus on the plan indicated by the key. They should be on the lookout for situations when this would be a good plan for them or another student to use. At the end of the day, the students will have a chance to tell about a time they were able to use the plan during the day. If they didn't see an opportunity to use the key plan themselves, they can tell about a situation when this would have been a good plan for someone else to have used. In this case, ask the students to describe the situation without using names. They could also describe a situation where they used the key plan in the past or when they might use the key plan in the future.

VARIATION

Pick a different key each morning for eight mornings and have the students write or draw about a time when they used that plan in handling a conflict, stating or showing what happened, what they did, and what they learned about handling conflicts from the experience.

SUPPLEMENTARY ACTIVITY #1 HANDOUT #1A

My STP Keys for Handling Conflicts

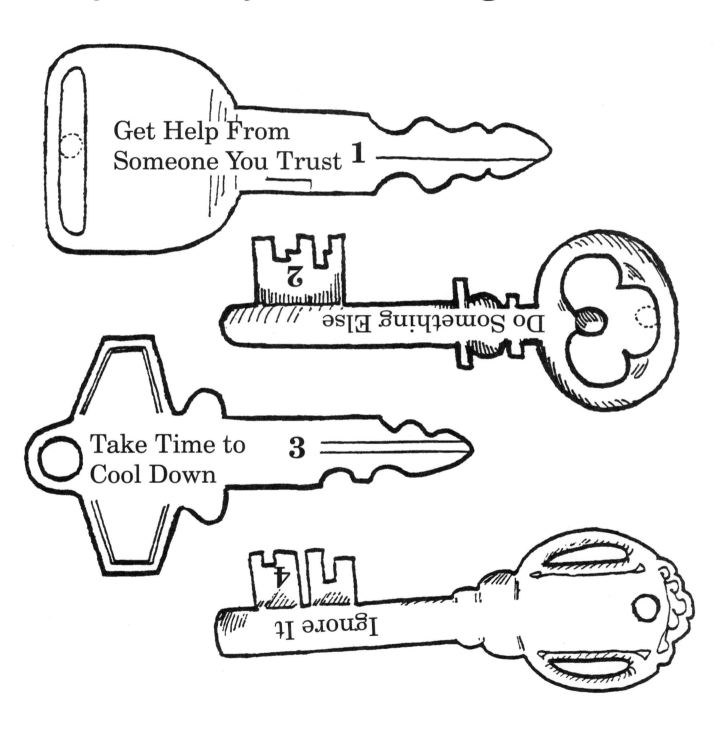

SUPPLEMENTARY ACTIVITY #1 HANDOUT #1B

My STP Keys for Handling Conflicts (continued)

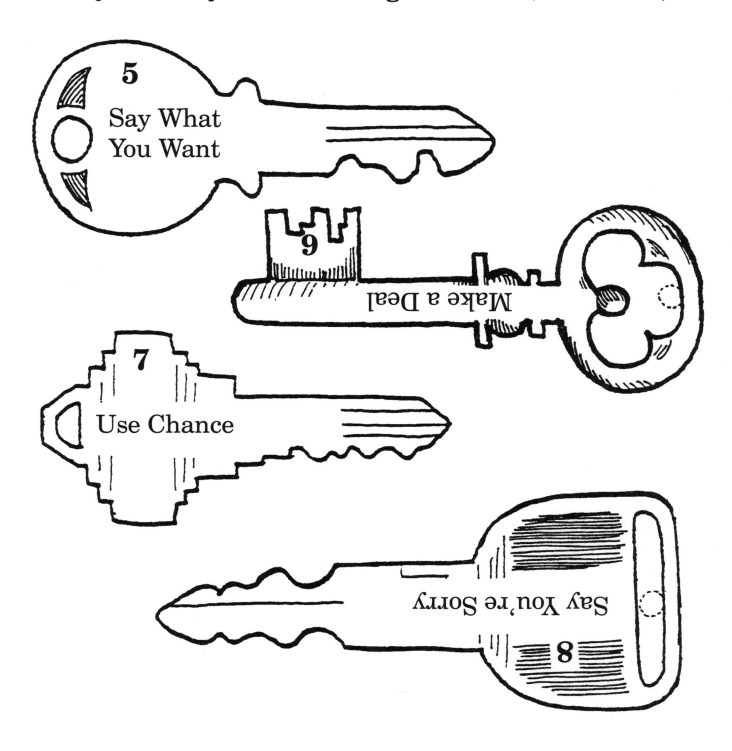

SUPPLEMENTARY ACTIVITY #2

Is Chance Fair?

Objective
Through experimentation with the chance activity of flipping a coin students will discover the fairness of using chance to decide a dispute.

Materials
Penny for each person in the class

Supplementary Activity #2 Handout, "Is Chance Fair? Tally Sheet" (one for each student pair)

Pencil for each student pair

Procedures
Divide students into pairs. Give each pair a coin and a copy of Supplementary Activity #2 Handout, "Is Chance Fair? Tally Sheet." Have one student in each pair flip the coin 50 times. The other student should put a mark in the "heads" or "tails" column on the tally sheet each time the coin is flipped to show how it landed. The students should then switch roles and repeat the activity. Once the coin has been flipped 100 times, the students should total up the number of marks in each column.

Have the student pairs report on their findings. How close were the scores? Explain to the students that while the totals for the two columns may not be **exactly** even, they can see from this experiment that they are **very close**. Point out that for some student pairs "heads" came up a little more, and for other student pairs "tails" came up a little more. Help the students to see that when you consider the totals for all of the class, flipping a coin is an even and fair way to settle disputes.

SUPPLEMENTARY ACTIVITY #2

Is Chance Fair?
Tally Sheet

Heads	Tails

Total _____   Total _____

Which column has more marks?   _____

How many more?   _____

For 100 flips, is that a lot more?   _____

Do you think chance is fair?   _____   Why or why not?
(Discuss this with the rest of your class.)

SUPPLEMENTARY ACTIVITY #3

Bear, Salmon, Mosquito Game

Objective   Students will use a game to master a fun chance technique and facilitate generalization to real-life situations.

Materials   Tape or chalk to make floor lines (optional)

Procedure   Before beginning the game, determine the "playing field" boundaries. If playing indoors, a basketball half-court may be used. If playing outdoors, use natural field boundaries such as trees, rocks, sidewalks, and so forth. In the center of the playing field make two parallel lines about four feet apart. At each end of the field mark a "home" line for each team.

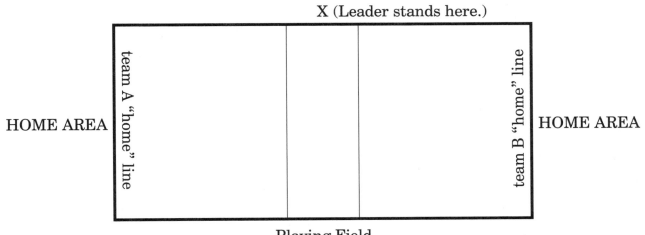

Playing Field

Divide the students into two teams. Line the two teams up facing each other along the two parallel lines at the center of the playing field. Explain to the students that each team will be going to their "home" area where they must decide whether they will all be bears, salmon, or mosquitoes. The bears will show that they are bears by raising their arms over their heads, forming claws with their hands, and growling. (Demonstrate for students and have them imitate.) The salmon will indicate that they are salmon by putting the palms of their hands together and making a zig-zag forward motion like a fish swimming. (Again, demonstrate for students and have them imitate the motion.) If students choose to be mosquitoes, they are to put the knuckle of their index, or pointer, finger up to their nose and extend their finger to form a "stinger" while making a buzzing sound. (Demonstrate and have students imitate.)

Remind the students how the Bear, Salmon, Mosquito chance activity works. Review which animal wins in each animal pair: Bears eat salmon, salmon eat mosquitoes, mosquitoes sting bears (spreading malaria).

To play the game, have the members of each team go to their "home" area and quietly decide which animal their team will be. Once both teams have chosen, the teams are to move forward and line up along their center line. The teacher, or a designated leader, will call out, "One, two, three, go!" When the players hear "go," they are to show which animal their team has chosen by making the motions and sounds of that animal. The teams must then **wait** until the leader shouts "Go!" again, at which point the players on the winning team are to try to tag the members of the other team before they can make it back across their "home" line. Any students who are tagged become members of the other team. Once again, each team decides what animal they are going to be, moves forward to their center line, and the game continues. Play continues in this fashion until time is up or until one team has captured all of the players from the other side.

SUPPLEMENTARY ACTIVITY #4

An "I'm Sorry" Note

When you've made a mistake and done something that's made another person upset, it can be hard to say "I'm sorry." Saying "I'm sorry" to someone you've upset is like giving the person a gift. Think of a person you need to apologize to. On the gift box below write the person the gift of an "I'm sorry" note. Then, if you feel like it, give the person the note.

SUPPLEMENTARY ACTIVITY #5

The STP Game
(Phase 3)

Objective   Students will add review and practice of the "pick a plan" step to the STP simulation game.

Materials   Big beach ball
Large traffic light poster (see Lesson 2, Supplementary Activity #4)
Situation cards
Whistle

Procedure   The first two phases of this game ("stop" and "think") were taught in Lesson 2. Refer to Supplementary Activity #4 in that lesson for details if you did not teach the game at that time. Phases 1 and 2 helped students to review and practice the "stop" and "think" STP steps. Phase 3 will now be added to help students review and practice the "pick a plan" step.

If you have not done so already, prepare for the STP simulation game by following the directions on Lesson 2, Supplementary Activity #4 Teacher Sheet, "Large Traffic Light Poster Instructions." You will also need to prepare the situation cards, if you have not done so already, by brainstorming "problem situations" with your class. Write each example given of a situation in which kids have conflicts with others on a 3" x 5" card. The cards will include such things as, "I was in line to get a drink and another student pushed in ahead of me." You may also wish to use some of the situations suggested in Lesson 3, Supplementary Activity #3, and Lesson 4, Supplementary Activity #2. (Even if you have situation cards from Lesson 2, you may wish to add more to the pile by brainstorming with your students.)

To play the game, students may either sit in a circle or be seated at their desks. The directions for Phase 3 follow.

PHASE 3

Instruct the students to throw the beach ball to one another at random around the circle or classroom. The "traffic attendant" (either you or a student appointed by you) attaches the red, yellow, or green light to the poster, blows the whistle to stop the activity, and then shows the poster to the class. The student who has the ball draws a situation card. After reading the card aloud, the student must state what he or she would say, think, or do at the step indicated by the traffic light. For the "pick a plan" step, in addition to saying the plan they would choose, students must also tell **why** they would choose that particular plan. (Discuss the plans chosen with the class, helping them to discern which are better choices in various situations.)

Once the ball is in play again, the "traffic attendant" may keep the traffic light on a given color or change it to another color before blowing the whistle again. Make sure the game keeps moving by not allowing too much time between light changes and whistle blows.

STP Your Way to School Game

Objective   Students will review the STP steps and apply them to various conflict situations.

Materials   Supplementary Activity #6 Transparency, "STP Your Way to School Game" (color game board Stop Card spaces red, Think Card spaces yellow, and Plan Card spaces green)

Stop Step game cards from Supplementary Activity #6 Teacher Sheets #1A–#1C (copy onto red paper and cut apart)

Think Step game cards from Supplementary Activity #6 Teacher Sheets #1D–#1F (copy onto yellow paper and cut apart)

Plan Step game cards from Supplementary Activity #6 Teacher Sheets #1G–#1I (copy onto green paper and cut apart)

Dice

Two differently colored or shaped tokens

Three small baskets or boxes for the game cards

Procedure   Divide the class into two teams and have the teammates sit near one another. Have the students on each team count off to establish an order among players for taking turns. Place Supplementary Activity #6 Transparency, "STP Your Way to School Game," on the overhead and put two differently colored or shaped tokens on the school bus "START" square. Give each team a die and choose three student helpers—one to keep score at his or her desk, one to stand at the overhead and move the team tokens, and one to be a timekeeper at his or her desk. (While students are getting accustomed to playing the game, you may want to give them 20 seconds to give answers; thereafter, reduce the time limit by half or according to the needs of your class.) Place the Stop, Think, and Plan game cards in three small baskets or boxes so that you will be able to walk to students' desks and offer them the cards to draw from when it is their turn. Note that the game board is set up so that the students first review the "stop" step, then progress on their way with the "think" step, and finally apply their knowledge of the "pick a plan" step to various conflict situations as they get closer to the finish (school).

To play, a member of each team will roll the team's die, and the team rolling the highest number will go first. Members of each team take turns rolling their die and moving their team's token from START to FINISH on the game board transparency. Players follow the instructions on the game board, moving ahead, going back, trading places with the other team's marker, or drawing a card according to the instructions.

When a team lands on a "Stop," "Think," or "Plan" square, the team member who rolled the die should draw a card from the appropriate box. You should read the card aloud and have the player who drew the card respond to the question on the card. For each correct response a player earns two points for his or her team. A player can choose to ask for help from a teammate if he or she is unsure about how to answer. In this case, the team scores half the allotted points (1 point). You will want to structure this help so that it won't be disruptive to the game, perhaps having potential "helpers" raise their hands to indicate that they know the answer. Also instruct teams that they will forfeit a point for whispering or offering unsolicited help. Teams may gain additional points by landing on the "Lucky 5" square. Landing on this square automatically gives the team five points.

The game ends when one team's token lands on the school "FINISH" square by exact count. The team with the most points at the end of play wins.

STP Your Way to School Game

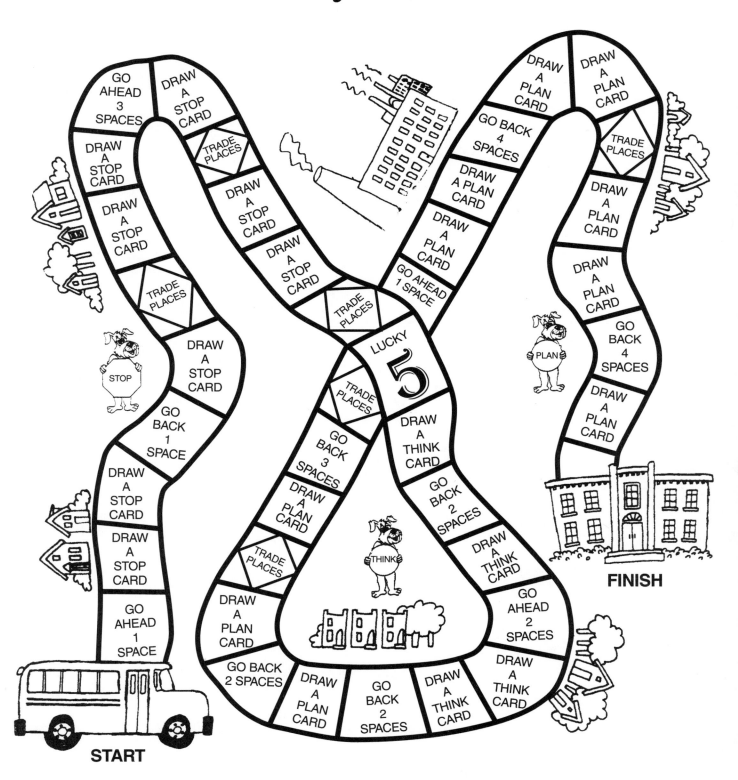

SUPPLEMENTARY ACTIVITY #6 TEACHER SHEET #1A

STOP STEP Game Cards

STP—Stop Step Your friend tells you that a girl is talking about you behind your back. She said she thought you were the dumbest person she'd ever met. The next day you see the girl walking down the street toward you. You feel your face getting red and your mind starts thinking of nasty things to say to her. What can you do to STOP yourself from giving her put-downs?	**STP—Stop Step** Your friends tease you when you volunteer in class. You feel yourself getting angry. What can you do to stop and calm yourself down?
STP—Stop Step You want to have your friend stay over on Friday night, but when you ask your parents, they say no. You feel yourself getting angry. What can you do to STOP and calm down so you won't blow up at them?	**STP—Stop Step** You are at a friend's house. She wants to watch TV and you want to play with some of her new toys. She says, "It's my house, and we're doing what I want to do." What do you do to STOP and calm yourself down?
STP—Stop Step Your mother takes you shopping to buy some new clothes, but she wants to make the decisions about what you should buy. That makes you mad. What can you do to STOP and calm yourself down?	**STP—Stop Step** Your friend says her parents won't allow you two to play together because they don't approve of your family. Before you get too angry and say something hurtful to your friend, what can you do to STOP and calm yourself down?

STOP STEP Game Cards (continued)

STP—Stop Step A classmate jumps on you and pushes you. Even though he's just playing around, it makes you mad. What do you do to STOP and calm yourself down?	**STP—Stop Step** A classmate teases you because you are wearing hand-me-downs. As you begin to feel angry, what do you do to STOP and calm yourself down?
STP—Stop Step You want to watch TV. Your mom tells you that you need to clean your room first. You hate cleaning your room. You feel that it's not fair that she makes you clean it when you were going to watch one of your favorite shows. You start to get mad. What can you do to STOP and calm yourself down?	**STP—Stop Step** You want to ride bikes and your friend wants to roller-skate. You start to get mad at each other. What do you do to STOP and calm yourself down?
STP—Stop Step You and another kid both want to sit by the window on the bus. The other kid pushes ahead of you and gets to the seat first. You clench your fists and want to hit him. What do you do to STOP and calm yourself down?	**STP—Stop Step** It's your turn to use one of the classroom balls at recess. As you are walking outside with it, another kid comes up and grabs it away from you, laughing. You feel all your muscles tighten and your face getting hot with anger. To STOP and calm yourself down, what do you do?

STOP STEP Game Cards (continued)

STP—Stop Step Your older sister is always on the phone. You want to use it and as you wait, you start to get mad because she talks so long. What do you do to STOP and calm yourself down?	**STP—Stop Step** Your 2-year-old sister grabs your homework paper and starts tearing it. You take it away from her. As you look at the ripped paper you start to get angry and you want to teach her a lesson. You make yourself STOP and calm down by doing what?
STP—Stop Step You are playing on the playground with your class during recess. Several kids from another class tease you by saying, "You're in the stupid class; you're retarded." What do you do to STOP and calm yourself down?	**STP—Stop Step** Your teacher says you can't have computer time because you were talking in class. You weren't talking, but the teacher thinks you were. You begin to get upset. What do you do to STOP and calm yourself down?
STP—Stop Step Your brother grabs the TV channel changer and switches the channel to a show he wants to watch. You are upset. What do you do to STOP and calm yourself down?	**STP—Stop Step**

SUPPLEMENTARY ACTIVITY #6 TEACHER SHEET #1D

THINK STEP Game Cards

### STP—Think Step A man pushes ahead of you at the sandwich counter in the grocery store and gets waited on first. You calm yourself down, breathing out the anger. Then you THINK _____.	### STP—Think Step Some of the kids in your classroom are laughing and making fun of another student. They think that hiding the student's trumpet when he's not looking would be a fun thing to do. They want you to be a part of this little trick. So they ask you to distract the student while they hide the trumpet. But you think this is mean. You stop yourself from getting angry and THINK _____.
### STP—Think Step One of your friends wants to play basketball at recess, but you and another friend what to jump rope. As you start to argue, you stop and calm yourself down. Then you THINK _____.	### STP—Think Step You've struck out for the third time during the baseball game. Other kids on your team say, "You're too wimpy to ever hit the ball." As you start to get angry you stop yourself and calm down. Then you THINK _____.
### STP—Think Step One of the kids in your class accuses you of stealing his favorite pencil. You didn't take it, and you are beginning to get angry because he keeps saying you did. You stop and calm yourself down. Then you THINK _____.	### STP—Think Step You're playing with your sister's toy. She hits you on the arm and grabs it back, saying, "Keep your hands off this. It's mine!" You are mad, but you stop and calm yourself down. Then you THINK _____.

THINK STEP Game Cards (continued)

### STP—Think Step You're playing a game of checkers with a kid when you see her move one of her checkers when she thought you weren't looking. When you tell her to put it back, she says that she never touched it and that the checker was there the whole time. You feel yourself getting angry. You tell yourself to "stop," and you take a deep breath and blow out the anger. Then you THINK _____.	### STP—Think Step You and a friend have talked about playing together at recess. But when you go out to the playground, your friend says he's decided to play with somebody else. You feel yourself getting angry at your friend. You stop your anger from growing by using the cool-down "stop" step. Then you THINK _____.
### STP—Think Step You are playing on the bars at recess. One of the kids keeps bragging about how much better she is than anyone else at doing stunts. As she talks, you feel yourself getting more and more angry. You stop your anger from growing by using the cool-down "stop" step. Then you THINK _____.	### STP—Think Step You and another kid in the class both want to be the first in line to go to music. You both rush toward the door, pushing each other out of the way. You are getting angry when you hear your teacher say, "Stop!" You listen to the teacher and manage to calm yourself down using the "stop" step. Then you THINK _____.
### STP—Think Step You are playing basketball and a ball hits you in the head. You turn around and see two kids pointing at you and laughing. You start getting mad but then stop and calm yourself down. You THINK _____.	### STP—Think Step You and a friend want to play Nintendo, but you can't agree on a game. You start to get mad but then stop and calm yourself down. Then you THINK _____.

THINK STEP Game Cards (continued)

STP—Think Step It's the first day at school and you've worn the glasses the eye doctor prescribed for you. Someone in your class says, "Hey, you have double eyes." This hurts your feelings and also makes you mad. Then you THINK _____.	**STP—Think Step** You and another kid both see a pencil on the floor. You are sure it is yours, but she grabs it and says it is hers. You get angry and want to grab it away from her. You stop and calm yourself down. Then you THINK _____.
STP—Think Step During free time in class you and a classmate both want to work on the same puzzle. You both begin arguing about who got it first. You stop yourself and calm down before you get too angry. Then you THINK _____.	**STP—Think Step** You are playing a card game with some other kids. You notice one of the kids cheating by looking at his neighbor's cards. You say something to him, but he calls you a liar. You calm yourself down by thinking "Stop!" and breathing out your anger. Then you THINK _____.
STP—Think Step A playground bully starts hogging the Big Toy, not letting anyone else play on it. You get mad but then calm yourself down. You THINK _____.	**STP—Think Step** You just received an F on a paper you thought was worth at least a C. You remember to stop and calm yourself down. Then you THINK _____.

PLAN STEP Game Cards

### STP—Plan Step Your soccer team just lost the game. Some of the players on the other team are making fun of your team. All of the players on your team are getting mad. You stop and calm yourself down. Then you think about what the smart thing to do is. You PICK A PLAN. Do you decide to ignore the teasing, make a deal (negotiate), or take time to cool down? Why?	### STP—Plan Step A classmate keeps mimicking you. She keeps on saying the same thing that you say. You feel yourself getting angry, but then you remember how to stop yourself and think. Then you PICK A PLAN. Is it to say you're sorry, say what you want, or get help? Why?
### STP—Plan Step You receive a note from a kid across the aisle saying that you're fat and ugly. You calm yourself down and think of what the smart thing to do is. You PICK A PLAN. Do you decide to tell them to stop, ignore it, or get help from someone you trust? Why?	### STP—Plan Step You're playing ball on the playground at recess. A big, tough kid comes up and takes your ball away. You feel yourself getting really angry and you want to slug the kid. You calm yourself down by using the "stop" step, then you think about whether to stay or walk away. You PICK A PLAN. Is it to use chance, to say what you want, or to go do something else? Why?
### STP—Plan Step Your friend criticizes you for not being able to do pull-ups on the horizontal bar. He makes fun of you and is not very nice to you. You are upset, but you stop and calm yourself down. Then you think of what the smart thing to do is. You PICK A PLAN. Do you decide to say what you want, go do something else, or use chance? Why?	### STP—Plan Step A friend borrows something of yours without asking. When you find out you start to get mad. Then you stop and calm yourself down. You think about what the smart thing to do is. Then you PICK A PLAN. Do you decide to use chance, ignore what your friend has done, or make a deal (negotiate)? Why?

PLAN STEP Game Cards (continued)

STP—Plan Step You accidentally trip a kid as you are both heading out the door to go home from school. The kid gets angry with you and starts to push you. That makes you mad and you are about to push back when you remember to stop and calm yourself down. You think about what the smart thing to do is. You PICK A PLAN. Do you decide to go do something else, get help, or say you're sorry? Why?	**STP—Plan Step** You are in the lunch line and someone cuts in front of you. You start to argue with the kid. The teacher hears you and sends you both to the back of the line. You are angry. You help yourself to cool down by using the "stop" step and then you think about what the smart thing to do is. You PICK A PLAN. Is it to say you're sorry, go do something else, or make a deal (negotiate)? Why?
STP—Plan Step You and a friend start talking about who can skate better. You feel yourself getting mad and want to say some mean things to her. Then you remember to stop and calm down. You think about what the smart thing to do is. Then you PICK A PLAN. Do you decide to make a deal (negotiate), say you're sorry for being wrong, or take time to cool down? Why?	**STP—Plan Step** You and your sister want to watch TV, but you want to watch different programs. You start to argue with each other, but then you remember to stop and calm down rather than keep getting angrier. You think about what the smart thing to do is and whether you want to stay or walk away. Then you PICK A PLAN. Do you ignore what your sister is saying or use chance? Why?
STP—Plan Step A kid who sits next to you is always poking you hard with his pencil. You've told him to stop, but he keeps doing it. You start to get mad but then you stop yourself and cool off. You think about what to do. You PICK A PLAN. Do you take time to cool down, go do something else, or get help from someone you trust? Why?	**STP—Plan Step** You know that you turned in your math paper, but your teacher says she doesn't have it. You start to get angry with her, but then you stop and calm down. You think about what the smart thing to do is. Then you PICK A PLAN. Do you make a deal (negotiate), take time to cool down, or ignore what the teacher is saying to you? Why?

PLAN STEP Game Cards (continued)

STP—Plan Step A classmate calls you names and teases you. You feel yourself getting angry, but then you stop and calm yourself down. You think about what the smart thing to do is. Then you PICK A PLAN. Do you decide to say what you want or take time to cool down? Why?	**STP—Plan Step** You are climbing the monkey bars during recess. A couple of kids yell at you to get off. "You're no good at climbing, Fatso. Get off," they say. You stop and calm yourself down. Then you think about what the smart thing to do is. You PICK A PLAN. Do you decide to say you're sorry, go do something else, or say what you want? Why?
STP—Plan Step Your brother had his allowance raised and you didn't. When you find out, you are mad, but you remember to stop and calm down and to think before you do anything. Then you PICK A PLAN. Do you decide to ignore what's happened, say what you want, or make a deal (negotiate) with your parents? Why?	**STP—Plan Step** A kid you know butts in when you are talking to other people and tries to change the subject. This has been happening often and really irritates you. You stay calm by using the "stop" step. Then you think about what the smart thing to do is. You PICK A PLAN. Do you decide to ignore the kid, go do something else, or say what you want? Why?
STP—Plan Step You think the Sonics are the best basketball team. Your friends think the Lakers are the best team. They start to gang up on you in an argument. You calm yourself down. You ask yourself what, the smart thing to do is. Then you PICK A PLAN. Do you decide to say you're sorry, ignore what they are saying, or say what you want? Why?	**STP—Plan Step**

SUPPLEMENTARY ACTIVITY #7

Using Chance

On the lines below, give examples of times when ***using chance*** could keep a small disagreement from turning into a big fight.

_____

_____

_____

_____

_____

Lesson 7

Putting It All Together

STP Review

Putting It All Together: STP Review

Objective   Students will review the STP steps for resolving conflicts, demonstrate an understanding of the concepts, and apply the concepts to real life situations.

Materials   Piece of 11" x 17" or larger thin paper on which you have written the words "Fun Times With Others"

Transparency #3 from Lesson 1 – "The §top Step"

Transparency #1 from Lesson 2 – "The Think Step"

Transparency #1 from Lesson 4 – "STP: §top, Think, and Pick a Plan"

Transparency #2 from Lesson 4 – "The Pick a Plan Step (What to Do If You §tay)"

Handout #1 – "My STP Calendar"

To the Teacher

This lesson ties together all of the components of the Stop, Think, and Pick a Plan approach to conflict resolution through the use of a story about a kid, Terry, who has a tough day because he doesn't know about using STP to solve conflicts with his friends and classmates. Students will have a chance to help Terry by suggesting what he could have done in each situation to de-escalate the conflict. They will then have an opportunity to role-play the situations from the story to gain further practice in using the STP process for resolving conflicts. The process of folding and unfolding the "Fun Times With Others" paper enhances the story.

It is important to encourage students to continue to use STP. Only as they practice the steps of this process in real-life situations will they begin to consistently handle their conflicts in successful ways. For this reason, their use of the "My STP Calendar" handout found at the end of this lesson is critical. By charting their use of STP each day on their calendars, students will be encouraged to use STP and be reinforced for doing so. If you are a specialist teaching this lesson, be sure to tell the students that you will be coming by periodically to look at their calendars and celebrate with them or congratulate them on the use of their new skills. The use of the supplementary activities that follow this lesson will also help to assure that students will transfer all that you taught them about handling conflict to real-life situations. In addition, they will gain further reinforcement if you send home the student letter that appears on page 18 after you have taught this lesson.

Lesson Presentation

LOOKING BACK

Who remembers the last two plans we talked about for solving arguments? *Allow for student response.* **Has anyone had a good experience using either chance or saying you're sorry?** *Allow for student response.* **Isn't it great to not waste time arguing or fighting with people when you can use the STP plans to solve problems? If you stop, think of a good plan, and use it when an argument starts, you can have fun for a whole recess instead of ruining things for yourself by turning the argument into a big fight. A lot of kids lose friends because they can't control their tempers.**

TERRY'S BAD DAY

Paper marked "Fun Times With Others"

Let me tell you a story about a boy named Terry. He's about your age. The thing that's most important to Terry is to have a good time with other kids. *Show the paper marked "Fun Times With Others."* **Let's say that this piece of paper stands for the fun times that Terry has with his classmates and friends. There are days when Terry has a lot of fun with other kids. But recently Terry had a whopper of a day where everything seemed to go wrong no matter which kids he was around. Here's what happened:**

Paragraph 1

Terry headed out to the bus stop to go to school in the morning. At the bus stop, he saw the friend he usually sits with on the bus. He ran over to talk with him. Then the bus pulled up. Both Terry and his friend wanted to be first to get on the bus. Terry pushed his friend out of the way so he could get on first. This made his friend really mad, and he walked right by where he and Terry usually sat and took a seat with another kid. Terry had to ride to school sitting next to a girl he didn't like. He missed out on the fun he usually had riding to school goofing off with his friend. There went some of his fun time for that day! *Fold the paper in half.*

Paragraph 2

When Terry got to his classroom and started getting ready for the day, he heard a girl say to another girl, "Terry likes Marsha!" This made Terry <u>so</u> mad that he grabbed the girl's lunch box to get even. The teacher saw him grabbing the lunch box and told him to give it back to the girl and go to his seat. He slammed the lunch box on her desk and called her a bad name before going to his seat. The teacher told Terry he would need to stay in for 5 minutes at recess as a punishment. There went more time that Terry could have spent with friends having fun! *Fold the paper in half again.*

Paragraph 3

Later that morning, Terry was working on his spelling. He had his feet out in the aisle and a classmate tripped on them. The kid gave Terry a dirty look and told him to get his feet out of the way. Terry said, "It's not my fault you're so clumsy." This made the kid really mad. When Terry finally made it out to recess after serving his 5 minutes, he tried to join a game, but the kid he tripped was one of the captains. The kid told all the other kids that Terry was a jerk and shouldn't get to play with them. Some of the kids went along with the captain and told Terry to get lost. Terry spent the rest of recess walking around with no one to play with. *Fold the paper in half again.* **Look how small Terry's fun time is getting!**

Paragraph 4

At lunchtime Terry usually sat with the friend he rode the bus with. But today that kid was sitting with some other kids at another table and didn't even save a place for Terry. Terry felt bad but ate his lunch in a hurry so he could get outside and play. Once outside, Terry went over to a Four Square game. The kids let Terry play, but then Terry started telling them that they weren't playing by the right rules. He kept trying to get them to play the game his way. This made the other kids so mad that they finally kicked Terry out of the game. Once again Terry lost time having fun with other kids. *Fold the paper in half again.*

Paragraph 5

After school Terry and a neighbor were playing in Terry's room. Terry's neighbor picked up a model plane that Terry's uncle had given him. Instead of telling the kid that he didn't like anybody playing with the plane, Terry blew up, yelled at the kid, and grabbed the plane. The kid suggested that they play checkers. Terry agreed and said, "I'm first." The kid said, "No, I want to be first." Terry dumped the board and said, "I don't want to play." The kid said, "I don't want to play with you either" and went home. *Fold the paper in half again.* Terry spent the rest of the evening by himself. Once again there was time lost that he could have spent having fun with someone.

After dinner Terry called up the friend he usually sat with on the bus and asked if he could spend the night on the weekend. His friend said he was going to sleep over with the kid that Terry tripped and called a name earlier in the day. Terry couldn't believe that his friend would turn him down for <u>that</u> kid.

When Terry went to bed that night, his face felt hot and some tears dripped down on his pillow. Terry felt that it had been a rotten day. *Hold up the folded piece of paper.* He had hardly had any fun with anybody.

Let's see if we can help Terry to have a better day tomorrow.

STP REVIEW

If Terry had known the STP steps for solving problems with other kids, he probably would have had a much better day. Before we help Terry figure out how to make tomorrow a better day than today was, let's review what we know about handling problems with others.

Who remembers what the "S" in STP stands for? *Allow for student response.* That's right, it stands for "Stop." *Show Transparency #3 from Lesson 1, "The <u>S</u>top Step," covering the bottom portion. Ask:* What do you do at the "stop" step to calm yourself down? *Allow for student re-*

sponse. Then uncover the bottom portion of the transparency. Say: **The "stop" step helps you to stop yourself from saying or doing something that will make the disagreement worse. It gives you time to cool down and be able to do the "T" part of STP.**

Lesson 2, Transp. #1

What does the "T" stand for in STP? *Allow for student response. Show Transparency #1 from Lesson 2, "The Think Step." Ask:* **What question do you ask yourself at this step?** *Allow for student response. Pointing to the words on the overhead, say:* **That's right. You ask yourself, "What's the smart thing to do, walk away or stay?"**

Lesson 4, Transp. #1

You're doing a great job! Now who can remember what the "P" stands for in STP? *Allow for student response. Show Transparency #1 from Lesson 4, "STP: Stop, Think, and Pick a Plan." Point to the appropriate places on the overhead and say:* **The last step in STP is to pick a plan. We've talked about eight different plans you can use if you are having an argument with someone. There are three plans to use if you decide to walk away from the situation and five plans you can use if you decide the smart thing to do is stay with the person and try to work things out. So, STP has three parts: STOP and calm down, THINK about whether the smart thing to do is to walk away or to stay, and PICK A PLAN you can use to make the situation better.**

Lesson 4, Transp. #2

Before we help Terry see how to have a better day tomorrow, let's review the eight plans we've learned. *Show Transparency #2 from Lesson 4, "The Pick a Plan Step (What to Do If You Stay)." Briefly review the eight plans with the students, asking for student volunteers to answer your questions and drawing names from the Popsicle stick can so that all students are thinking and preparing themselves to answer. Point to the appropriate places on the transparency and say something like:*

There are three plans that you can use if you decide that the smart thing to do is walk away from a situation. One is to get help from someone you trust. When would this be a good plan to use? *Allow for student response.* **Good! Whenever you are in danger of being hurt, you should get help.**

Who can think of a time when it would be a good idea to go do something else? *Allow for student response.*

And when would it be smart to take time to cool down? That is, when might the "stop" step not be enough and you might need more time to cool off? *Allow for student response. Then ask:* **What are some things you could do to help yourself calm down?** *Allow for student response.*

Let's move now to the plans you can use if you decide that the smart thing to do is stay, not walk away. Who can describe a time when the best plan might be to just ignore what someone else is doing? *Allow for student response.*

Who can think of a time when you might use the plan of telling someone what you want? *Allow for student response.*

Let's talk about making a deal. What's another word for this plan? *Allow for student response. Say:* **That's right. It's "negotiate." Does anyone remember one of the three ways to make a deal?** *Allow for student responses until the students have stated all three.*

There are only two more plans to go! What are some ways you can use chance to solve a problem? Has anybody tried any of these ways? *Allow for student response.*

Finally, there's the "say you're sorry" plan. When is a good time to use this plan? *Allow for student response.*

TERRY'S BETTER DAY

Now we're ready to help Terry with his day. Remember, everyone has disagreements with other people. Disagreements are a normal part of life. But by using the STP steps to handle conflicts, arguments can often be settled before they turn into big fights. Terry had several disagreements during his day. Let's help him use STP to find a plan for each one of his disagreements, a plan that could have stopped those disagreements from messing up his day.

Hold up the "Fun Times With Others" paper, which has been folded in half five times. Say: **This little piece of paper represents all the fun time Terry had left at the end of the day. Let's see if we can help Terry make his fun time grow.**

Read paragraph 1 of "Terry's Bad Day" to the students. Then ask the following questions to get students thinking about conflict resolution plans Terry could have used. Throughout this review, vary calling on volunteers and drawing Popsicle sticks so that all students will remain on the alert. Begin by asking: **When was the first time Terry should have used the "stop" and "think" plans?** *(When he and his friend both wanted to get on the bus first.)* **What plan could Terry have used at this moment that would have stopped a small problem from turning into a bigger one?** *Accept "make a deal" or "say what you want" and unfold the paper one time.*

Read paragraph 2. **What could Terry have done to save himself trouble when he overheard what the girl said?** *Accept "take time to cool down," "ignore it," or "say what you want." Unfold the paper once more.*

Read paragraph 3. **What would have been a smart thing for Terry to do when the boy tripped over Terry's foot?** *Accept "say you're sorry" or "ignore it" and unfold the paper once again.*

Read paragraph 4. **What should Terry have done when the kids wanted to keep using their rules for the Four Square game rather than change over to Terry's rules?** *Accept "go do something else" or "make a deal." Unfold the paper again and say:* **"Wow! Terry's fun time with other kids is really increasing now that he's using smart plans to keep little disagreements from turning into big ones.**

Read paragraph 5. **What would have been a smart thing for Terry to do when the neighbor kid picked up his model plane?** *Accept "say what you want" or "make a deal."* **If you were Terry, what would you have done when both you and the other kid wanted to go first in checkers?** *Accept "use chance" or "make a deal." Unfold the paper one last time and say:* **Look! Terry could have had a whole day of fun with** other kids if he had just known about stopping, thinking of the smart thing to do, and picking a good plan!

ROLE-PLAY PRACTICE

Just for fun, let's try role-playing some of the things that happened to Terry. Some of you can take turns being Terry. Some of you can play the kids he got into disagreements with. And some of you can play yourself coaching Terry on a good plan for him to use so he doesn't ruin his friendships. Let me show you what I mean. *Start the role-playing by calling on two students to act out the bus incident described in paragraph 1. After the students start to argue about who's going to get on the bus first and Terry pushes his friend, model being the coach. Using a loud whisper, urge Terry to make a deal by suggesting he and his friend take turns getting on the bus first. Continue with the other role-plays, having students play all the parts.*

WRAP-UP

You've done such a nice job role-playing. In real life, of course, when you're actually involved in disputes, it's a lot harder to handle disagreements well. Learning to control your temper can be one of the hardest things to do. Just remembering to stop and calm down is hard for most people, let alone knowing whether you should walk away or stay when you're having a disagreement with someone.

Picking a smart plan can happen only after you have calmed yourself down in an argument. And deciding which plan will best solve the problem takes a lot of practice. Don't get discouraged if you don't handle every argument perfectly. Learning to use STP is kind of like learning to play the piano. You have to keep practicing to get good at it.

Handout #1 *Give students Handout #1, "My STP Calendar," and say:* I'd like you to keep a current copy of this little calendar on the corner of your desk or taped to the inside of your STP folder. We're going to use the calendar to remind ourselves to use STP. Here's how the activity works: Let's say that it's Tuesday and at lunch recess you and another kid both want to use the same ball and you start to argue. Then you remember to stop, think, and pick a plan. The plan you pick is "make a deal." You both share the ball and you're still friends. At the end of the day, you would get out your STP calendar and draw a big smiley face in the Tuesday box, just like the one shown for a great day.

Now let's say it's Wednesday and I say, "Get out your STP calendars and fill in your face for the day!" You think back over your day and you can't remember any disagreements that came up. What should you do? Just draw a face that doesn't look really happy or really sad, like the one shown for a so-so day.

O.K., now it's Friday. And you blew up at a kid when she didn't play a game the way you thought she should. You thought about STP, but it felt so good to blow up and call her a bunch of names that you just let yourself do it. The girl's still mad at you and what felt good before now feels kind of embarrassing. You blew it. What kind of face do you think you ought to draw in the Friday box? *Allow for student response.*

One of the ways people get a good habit going is to ask themselves every day how they're doing and to give themselves credit when they remember to do the smart thing. I'll just bet that if you ask yourselves every day for 4 weeks how you're doing on STP you'll be the most mature kids in the school when it comes to handling disagreements with other kids.

Review the STP lessons by asking the students to complete the following sentence stems:

- I'm glad you taught us . . .

- A time I will use what I have learned is . . .

- One of the plans I like best is . . .

- What I'll remember most is . . .

- **The thing I like best about the STP lessons is . . .**

- **What I think I'll use the most from what I've learned is . . .**

- **I know this stuff works because . . .**

SUPPLEMENTARY ACTIVITIES

Use the supplementary activities that follow this lesson to reinforce the lesson concepts.

- *Stop, Think, and Pick a Plan Bingo*
  (Supplementary Activity #1)

- *STP Match-Up*
  (Supplementary Activity #2)

- *Stop, Think, and Pick a Plan! Cube Roll*
  (Supplementary Activity #3)

- *Fishing for a Plan*
  (Supplementary Activity #4)

- *STP Mobile*
  (Supplementary Activity #5)

HANDOUT #1

My STP Calendar

Name: _____   Date: _____

Great Day   So-So Day   I Need Improvement

Monday	Tuesday	Wednesday	Thursday	Friday

My STP Calendar

Name: _____   Date: _____

Great Day   So-So Day   I Need Improvement

Monday	Tuesday	Wednesday	Thursday	Friday

SUPPLEMENTARY ACTIVITY #1

<u>S</u>top, <u>T</u>hink, and Pick a <u>P</u>lan Bingo

Objective   Students will review the behaviors they can use in the STP process.

Materials   Supplementary Activity #1 Teacher Sheet, "<u>S</u>top, <u>T</u>hink, and Pick a <u>P</u>lan Bing<u>o</u> Game Pieces" (cut apart and laminate if desired)

Supplementary Activity #1 Game Card #1-#30, "<u>S</u>top, <u>T</u>hink, and Pick a <u>P</u>lan Bing<u>o</u>" (copied on colorful paper and laminated)

Game tokens for each player (approximately 15 per student); these can be small squares of paper or edible tokens, such as candy, nuts, popped corn, or cereal that can be eaten at the end of the game

Basket or box for game pieces

Procedure   Give each student a game card and 15 tokens. Tell the students what spaces (five in a row, four corners, an "X," etc.) need to be covered to win the game. Because all STP actions are written on each game card, covering all the spaces for a blackout is not an option. (Everyone would get Bingo.) To begin the game, draw a game piece from the box or basket and read it aloud to the class. Explain that all students will have each STP behavior on their game board. Wait until every student has found and covered the space containing the behavior you have read before selecting and reading the next game piece. If a student has trouble finding a space, other students can assist the student; it will not jeopardize their chances of winning. Once a student has covered the required spaces, he or she must call out "STP-GO" to win.

SUPPLEMENTARY ACTIVITY #1 TEACHER SHEET

<u>S</u>top, <u>T</u>hink, and Pick a <u>P</u>lan
Bing<u>o</u> Game Pieces

Cut apart the following game pieces, laminate them (if desired), and place them in a basket or box so you can draw them randomly.

Say what you want.	Go do something else.	Ignore it.	Apologize.	Take turns.
Think: What's the smart thing to do?	Rock, Paper, Scissors.	Take a deep breath.	Negotiate.	Ask yourself, Will I get hurt?
Stop and cool down.	Make a deal.	Say you're sorry.	Share	Get help from someone you trust.
Stay and talk it out.	Tell the person to stop.	Use chance.	Say or think "Stop."	Swap.
Blow out your anger.	Ask yourself, Will I get in trouble?	Think: Should I walk away or stay?	**S**top, **T**hink, and Pick a **P**lan.	Draw straws.

SUPPLEMENTARY ACTIVITY #1 GAME CARD #1

<u>S</u>top, <u>T</u>hink, and Pick a <u>P</u>lan Bin<u>go</u>

	S	T	P-	G	O
1	Go do something else.	Ignore it.	Think: Should I walk away or stay?	**S**top, **T**hink, and Pick a **P**lan.	Say what you want.
2	Rock, Paper, Scissors.	Take a deep breath.	Apologize.	Take turns.	Think: What's the smart thing to do?
3	Make a deal.	Draw straws.	Negotiate.	Ask yourself, Will I get hurt?	Stop and cool down.
4	Tell the person to stop.	Say you're sorry.	Share.	Get help from someone you trust.	Stay and talk it out.
5	Ask yourself, Will I get in trouble?	Use chance.	Say or think "Stop."	Swap.	Blow out your anger.

SUPPLEMENTARY ACTIVITY #1 GAME CARD #2

<u>S</u>top, <u>T</u>hink, and Pick a <u>P</u>lan Bing<u>o</u>

	S	T	P-	G	O
1	Think: What's the smart thing to do?	Go do something else.	Ignore it.	Think: Should I walk away or stay?	**S**top, **T**hink, and Pick a **P**lan.
2	Stop and cool down.	Rock, Paper, Scissors.	Take a deep breath.	Apologize.	Take turns.
3	Stay and talk it out.	Make a deal.	Draw straws.	Negotiate.	Ask yourself, Will I get hurt?
4	Blow out your anger.	Tell the person to stop.	Say you're sorry.	Share.	Get help from someone you trust.
5	Say what you want.	Ask yourself, Will I get in trouble?	Use chance.	Say or think "Stop."	Swap.

SUPPLEMENTARY ACTIVITY #1 GAME CARD #3

<u>S</u>top, <u>T</u>hink, and Pick a <u>P</u>lan Bin<u>go</u>

	S	T	P-	G	O
1	Swap.	Think: What's the smart thing to do?	Go do something else.	Ignore it.	Think: Should I walk away or stay?
2	**S**top, **T**hink, and Pick a **P**lan.	Stop and cool down.	Rock, Paper, Scissors.	Take a deep breath.	Apologize.
3	Take turns.	Stay and talk it out.	Make a deal.	Draw straws.	Negotiate.
4	Ask yourself, Will I get hurt?	Blow out your anger.	Tell the person to stop.	Say you're sorry.	Share.
5	Get help from someone you trust.	Say what you want.	Ask yourself, Will I get in trouble?	Use chance.	Say or think "Stop."

SUPPLEMENTARY ACTIVITY #1 GAME CARD #4

Stop, Think, and Pick a Plan Bingo

	S	T	P-	G	O
1	Think: What's the smart thing to do?	Go do something else.	Ignore it.	Think: Should I walk away or stay?	Swap.
2	Stop and cool down.	Rock, Paper, Scissors.	Take a deep breath.	Apologize.	**S**top, **T**hink, and Pick a **P**lan.
3	Stay and talk it out.	Make a deal.	Draw straws.	Negotiate.	Take turns.
4	Blow out your anger.	Tell the person to stop.	Say you're sorry.	Share.	Ask yourself, Will I get hurt?
5	Say what you want.	Ask yourself, Will I get in trouble?	Use chance.	Say or think "Stop."	Get help from someone you trust.

SUPPLEMENTARY ACTIVITY #1 GAME CARD #5

<u>S</u>top, <u>T</u>hink, and Pick a <u>P</u>lan Bin<u>go</u>

	S	T	P-	G	O
1	Swap.	Think: What's the smart thing to do?	Go do something else.	Ignore it.	Think: Should I walk away or stay?
2	**S**top, **T**hink, and Pick a **P**lan.	Stop and cool down.	Rock, Paper, Scissors.	Take a deep breath.	Apologize.
3	Take turns.	Stay and talk it out.	Make a deal.	Draw straws.	Negotiate.
4	Ask yourself, Will I get hurt?	Blow out your anger.	Tell the person to stop.	Say you're sorry.	Share.
5	Get help from someone you trust.	Say what you want.	Ask yourself, Will I get in trouble?	Use chance.	Say or think "Stop."

<u>S</u>top, <u>T</u>hink, and Pick a <u>P</u>lan Bin<u>go</u>

	S	T	P-	G	O
1	Think: Should I walk away or stay?	Swap.	Think: What's the smart thing to do?	Go do something else.	Ignore it.
2	Apologize.	**S**top, **T**hink, and Pick a **P**lan.	Stop and cool down.	Rock, Paper, Scissors.	Take a deep breath.
3	Negotiate.	Take turns.	Stay and talk it out.	Make a deal.	Draw straws.
4	Share.	Ask yourself, Will I get hurt?	Blow out your anger.	Tell the person to stop.	Say you're sorry.
5	Say or think "Stop."	Get help from someone you trust.	Say what you want.	Ask yourself, Will I get in trouble?	Use chance.

SUPPLEMENTARY ACTIVITY #1 GAME CARD #7

<u>S</u>top, <u>T</u>hink, and Pick a <u>P</u>lan Bin<u>go</u>

	S	T	P-	G	O
1	Ignore it.	Think: Should I walk away or stay?	Swap.	Think: What's the smart thing to do?	Go do something else.
2	Take a deep breath.	Apologize.	**S**top, **T**hink, and Pick a **P**lan.	Stop and cool down.	Rock, Paper, Scissors.
3	Draw straws.	Negotiate.	Take turns.	Stay and talk it out.	Make a deal.
4	Say you're sorry.	Share.	Ask yourself, Will I get hurt?	Blow out your anger.	Tell the person to stop.
5	Use chance.	Say or think "Stop."	Get help from someone you trust.	Say what you want.	Ask yourself, Will I get in trouble?

SUPPLEMENTARY ACTIVITY #1 GAME CARD #8

<u>S</u>top, <u>T</u>hink, and Pick a <u>P</u>lan Bin<u>go</u>

	S	**T**	**P-**	**G**	**O**
1	Go do something else.	Ignore it.	Think: Should I walk away or stay?	Swap.	Think: What's the smart thing to do?
2	Rock, Paper, Scissors.	Take a deep breath.	Apologize.	**S**top, **T**hink, and Pick a **P**lan.	Stop and cool down.
3	Make a deal.	Draw straws.	Negotiate.	Take turns.	Stay and talk it out.
4	Tell the person to stop.	Say you're sorry.	Share.	Ask yourself, Will I get hurt?	Blow out your anger.
5	Ask yourself, Will I get in trouble?	Use chance.	Say or think "Stop."	Get help from someone you trust.	Say what you want.

SUPPLEMENTARY ACTIVITY #1 GAME CARD #9

<u>S</u>top, <u>T</u>hink, and Pick a <u>P</u>lan Bin<u>go</u>

	S	T	P-	G	O
1	Rock, Paper, Scissors.	Ignore it.	Think: Should I walk away or stay?	**S**top, **T**hink, and Pick a **P**lan.	Think: What's the smart thing to do?
2	Make a deal.	Take a deep breath.	Negotiate.	Swap.	Stay and talk it out.
3	Tell the person to stop.	Use chance.	Apologize.	Take turns.	Stop and cool down.
4	Go do something else.	Draw straws.	Share.	Ask yourself, Will I get hurt?	Blow out your anger.
5	Ask yourself, Will I get in trouble?	Say you're sorry.	Say or think "Stop."	Get help from someone you trust.	Say what you want.

SUPPLEMENTARY ACTIVITY #1 GAME CARD #10

Stop, Think, and Pick a Plan Bingo

	S	T	P-	G	O
1	Think: What's the smart thing to do?	Rock, Paper, Scissors.	Ignore it.	Think: Should I walk away or stay?	Stop, Think, and Pick a Plan.
2	Stay and talk it out.	Make a deal.	Take a deep breath.	Negotiate.	Swap.
3	Stop and cool down.	Tell the person to stop.	Use chance.	Apologize.	Take turns.
4	Blow out your anger.	Go do something else.	Draw straws.	Share.	Ask yourself, Will I get hurt?
5	Say what you want.	Ask yourself, Will I get in trouble?	Say you're sorry.	Say or think "Stop."	Get help from someone you trust.

SUPPLEMENTARY ACTIVITY #1 GAME CARD #11

Stop, Think, and Pick a Plan Bingo

	S	T	P-	G	O
1	**S**top, **T**hink, and Pick a **P**lan.	Think: What's the smart thing to do?	Rock, Paper, Scissors.	Ignore it.	Think: Should I walk away or stay?
2	Swap.	Stay and talk it out.	Make a deal.	Take a deep breath.	Negotiate.
3	Take turns.	Stop and cool down.	Tell the person to stop.	Use chance.	Apologize.
4	Ask yourself, Will I get hurt?	Blow out your anger.	Go do something else.	Draw straws.	Share.
5	Get help from someone you trust.	Say what you want.	Ask yourself, Will I get in trouble?	Say you're sorry.	Say or think "Stop."

SUPPLEMENTARY ACTIVITY #1 GAME CARD #12

<u>S</u>top, <u>T</u>hink, and Pick a <u>P</u>lan Bingo

	S	T	P-	G	O
1	Think: Should I walk away or stay?	**S**top, **T**hink, and Pick a **P**lan.	Think: What's the smart thing to do?	Rock, Paper, Scissors.	Ignore it.
2	Negotiate.	Swap.	Stay and talk it out.	Make a deal.	Take a deep breath.
3	Apologize.	Take turns.	Stop and cool down.	Tell the person to stop.	Use chance.
4	Share.	Ask yourself, Will I get hurt?	Blow out your anger.	Go do something else.	Draw straws.
5	Say or think "Stop."	Get help from someone you trust.	Say what you want.	Ask yourself, Will I get in trouble?	Say you're sorry.

SUPPLEMENTARY ACTIVITY #1 GAME CARD #13

<u>S</u>top, <u>T</u>hink, and Pick a <u>P</u>lan Bing<u>o</u>

	S	T	P-	G	O
1	Ignore it.	Think: Should I walk away or stay?	**S**top, **T**hink, and Pick a **P**lan.	Think: What's the smart thing to do?	Rock, Paper, Scissors.
2	Take a deep breath.	Negotiate.	Swap.	Stay and talk it out.	Make a deal.
3	Use chance.	Apologize.	Take turns.	Stop and cool down.	Tell the person to stop.
4	Draw straws.	Share.	Ask yourself, Will I get hurt?	Blow out your anger.	Go do something else.
5	Say you're sorry.	Say or think "Stop."	Get help from someone you trust.	Say what you want.	Ask yourself, Will I get in trouble?

SUPPLEMENTARY ACTIVITY #1 GAME CARD #14

<u>S</u>top, <u>T</u>hink, and Pick a <u>P</u>lan Bin<u>go</u>

	S	T	P-	G	O
1	Ignore it.	Think: Should I walk away or stay?	**S**top, **T**hink, and Pick a **P**lan.	Rock, Paper, Scissors.	Make a deal.
2	Take a deep breath.	Negotiate.	Swap.	Think: What's the smart thing to do?	Tell the person to stop.
3	Use chance.	Apologize.	Ask yourself, Will I get hurt?	Stay and talk it out.	Go do something else.
4	Draw straws.	Say you're sorry.	Get help from someone you trust.	Take turns.	Ask yourself, Will I get in trouble?
5	Share.	Say or think "Stop."	Blow out your anger.	Say what you want.	Stop and cool down.

SUPPLEMENTARY ACTIVITY #1 GAME CARD #15

<u>S</u>top, <u>T</u>hink, and Pick a <u>P</u>lan Bin<u>go</u>

	S	T	P-	G	O
1	Say what you want.	Go do something else.	Ignore it.	Apologize.	Take turns.
2	Think: What's the smart thing to do?	Rock, Paper, Scissors.	Take a deep breath.	Negotiate.	Ask yourself, Will I get hurt?
3	Stop and cool down.	Make a deal.	Say you're sorry.	Share.	Get help from someone you trust.
4	Stay and talk it out.	Tell the person to stop.	Use chance.	Say or think "Stop."	Swap.
5	Blow out your anger.	Ask yourself, Will I get in trouble?	Think: Should I walk away or stay?	**S**top, **T**hink, and Pick a **P**lan.	Draw straws.

SUPPLEMENTARY ACTIVITY #1 GAME CARD #16

<u>S</u>top, <u>T</u>hink, and Pick a <u>P</u>lan Bin<u>go</u>

	S	T	P-	G	O
1	Make a deal.	Ignore it.	Think: Should I walk away or stay?	**S**top, **T**hink, and Pick a **P**lan.	Take turns.
2	Tell the person to stop.	Rock, Paper, Scissors.	Take a deep breath.	Negotiate.	Think: What's the smart thing to do?
3	Go do something else.	Use chance.	Apologize.	Ask yourself, Will I get hurt?	Stay and talk it out.
4	Ask yourself, Will I get in trouble?	Draw straws.	Say you're sorry.	Get help from someone you trust.	Swap.
5	Stop and cool down.	Share.	Say or think "Stop."	Blow out your anger.	Say what you want.

SUPPLEMENTARY ACTIVITY #1 GAME CARD #17

<u>S</u>top, <u>T</u>hink, and Pick a <u>P</u>lan Bin<u>go</u>

	S	T	P-	G	O
1	Rock, Paper, Scissors.	Make a deal.	Ignore it.	Think: Should I walk away or stay?	**S**top, **T**hink, and Pick a **P**lan.
2	Think: What's the smart thing to do?	Tell the person to stop.	Take a deep breath.	Negotiate.	Swap.
3	Stay and talk it out.	Go do something else.	Use chance.	Apologize.	Ask yourself, Will I get hurt?
4	Take turns.	Ask yourself, Will I get in trouble?	Draw straws.	Say you're sorry.	Get help from someone you trust.
5	Say what you want.	Stop and cool down.	Share.	Say or think "Stop."	Blow out your anger.

SUPPLEMENTARY ACTIVITY #1 GAME CARD #18

Stop, Think, and Pick a Plan Bingo

	S	T	P-	G	O
1	Rock, Paper, Scissors.	Make a deal.	Ignore it.	Think: Should I walk away or stay?	Stop, Think, and Pick a Plan.
2	Think: What's the smart thing to do?	Tell the person to stop.	Take a deep breath.	Negotiate.	Swap.
3	Stay and talk it out.	Go do something else.	Use chance.	Apologize.	Ask yourself, Will I get hurt?
4	Take turns.	Ask yourself, Will I get in trouble?	Draw straws.	Say you're sorry.	Get help from someone you trust.
5	Say what you want.	Stop and cool down.	Share.	Say or think "Stop."	Blow out your anger.

SUPPLEMENTARY ACTIVITY #1 GAME CARD #19

<u>S</u>top, <u>T</u>hink, and Pick a <u>P</u>lan Bin<u>go</u>

	S	T	P-	G	O
1	**S**top, **T**hink, and Pick a **P**lan.	Rock, Paper, Scissors.	Make a deal.	Ignore it.	Think: Should I walk away or stay?
2	Swap.	Think: What's the smart thing to do?	Tell the person to stop.	Take a deep breath.	Negotiate.
3	Ask yourself, Will I get hurt?	Stay and talk it out.	Go do something else.	Use chance.	Apologize.
4	Get help from someone you trust.	Take turns.	Ask yourself, Will I get in trouble?	Draw straws.	Say you're sorry.
5	Blow out your anger.	Say what you want.	Stop and cool down.	Share.	Say or think "Stop."

SUPPLEMENTARY ACTIVITY #1 GAME CARD #20

<u>S</u>top, <u>T</u>hink, and Pick a <u>P</u>lan Bin<u>go</u>

	S	T	P-	G	O
1	Think: Should I walk away or stay?	**S**top, **T**hink, and Pick a **P**lan.	Rock, Paper, Scissors.	Say you're sorry.	Take a deep breath.
2	Negotiate.	Swap.	Think: What's the smart thing to do?	Make a deal.	Use chance.
3	Tell the person to stop.	Ask yourself, Will I get hurt?	Ignore it.	Go do something else.	Draw straws.
4	Apologize.	Get help from someone you trust.	Stay and talk it out.	Ask yourself, Will I get in trouble?	Say what you want.
5	Say or think "Stop."	Blow out your anger.	Take turns.	Stop and cool down.	Share.

SUPPLEMENTARY ACTIVITY #1 GAME CARD #21

<u>S</u>top, <u>T</u>hink, and Pick a <u>P</u>lan Bin<u>go</u>

	S	T	P-	G	O
1	Take a deep breath.	Think: Should I walk away or stay?	**S**top, **T**hink, and Pick a **P**lan.	Rock, Paper, Scissors.	Say you're sorry.
2	Use chance.	Negotiate.	Swap.	Think: What's the smart thing to do?	Make a deal.
3	Draw straws.	Ask yourself, Will I get hurt?	Tell the person to stop.	Ignore it.	Go do something else.
4	Say what you want.	Apologize.	Get help from someone you trust.	Stay and talk it out.	Ask yourself, Will I get in trouble?
5	Share.	Say or think "Stop."	Blow out your anger.	Take turns.	Stop and cool down.

SUPPLEMENTARY ACTIVITY #1 GAME CARD #22

<u>S</u>top, <u>T</u>hink, and Pick a <u>P</u>lan Bing<u>o</u>

	S	T	P-	G	O
1	Say you're sorry.	Take a deep breath.	Think: Should I walk away or stay?	**S**top, **T**hink, and Pick a **P**lan.	Rock, Paper, Scissors.
2	Make a deal.	Use chance.	Negotiate.	Swap.	Think: What's the smart thing to do?
3	Go do something else.	Draw straws.	Tell the person to stop.	Ask yourself, Will I get hurt?	Ignore it.
4	Ask yourself, Will I get in trouble?	Say what you want.	Apologize.	Get help from someone you trust.	Stay and talk it out.
5	Stop and cool down.	Share.	Say or think "Stop."	Blow out your anger.	Take turns.

SUPPLEMENTARY ACTIVITY #1 GAME CARD #23

<u>S</u>top, <u>T</u>hink, and Pick a <u>P</u>lan Bin<u>go</u>

	S	T	P-	G	O
1	Rock, Paper, Scissors.	Say you're sorry.	Take a deep breath.	Think: Should I walk away or stay?	**S**top, **T**hink, and Pick a **P**lan.
2	Think: What's the smart thing to do?	Make a deal.	Use chance.	Negotiate.	Swap.
3	Ignore it.	Go do something else.	Draw straws.	Tell the person to stop.	Ask yourself, Will I get hurt?
4	Stay and talk it out.	Ask yourself, Will I get in trouble?	Say what you want.	Apologize.	Get help from someone you trust.
5	Take turns.	Stop and cool down.	Share.	Say or think "Stop."	Blow out your anger.

SUPPLEMENTARY ACTIVITY #1 GAME CARD #24

<u>S</u>top, <u>T</u>hink, and Pick a <u>P</u>lan Bin<u>go</u>

	S	**T**	**P-**	**G**	**O**
1	**S**top, **T**hink, and Pick a **P**lan.	Rock, Paper, Scissors.	Say you're sorry.	Take a deep breath.	Think: Should I walk away or stay?
2	Swap.	Think: What's the smart thing to do?	Make a deal.	Use chance.	Negotiate.
3	Ask yourself, Will I get hurt?	Ignore it.	Go do something else.	Draw straws.	Tell the person to stop.
4	Get help from someone you trust.	Stay and talk it out.	Ask yourself, Will I get in trouble?	Say what you want.	Apologize.
5	Blow out your anger.	Take turns.	Stop and cool down.	Share.	Say or think "Stop."

SUPPLEMENTARY ACTIVITY #1 GAME CARD #25

<u>S</u>top, <u>T</u>hink, and Pick a <u>P</u>lan Bing<u>o</u>

	S	T	P-	G	O
1	**S**top, **T**hink, and Pick a **P**lan.	Apologize.	Get help from someone you trust.	Take a deep breath.	Think: Should I walk away or stay?
2	Ask yourself, Will I get hurt?	Think: What's the smart thing to do?	Say you're sorry.	Use chance.	Negotiate.
3	Blow out your anger.	Ignore it.	Go do something else.	Swap.	Tell the person to stop.
4	Make a deal.	Stay and talk it out.	Ask yourself, Will I get in trouble?	Draw straws.	Rock, Paper, Scissors.
5	Say what you want.	Take turns.	Stop and cool down.	Share.	Say or think "Stop."

SUPPLEMENTARY ACTIVITY #1 GAME CARD #26

<u>S</u>top, <u>T</u>hink, and Pick a <u>P</u>lan Bin<u>go</u>

	S	T	P-	G	O
1	Think: Should I walk away or stay?	**S**top, **T**hink, and Pick a **P**lan.	Apologize.	Get help from someone you trust.	Take a deep breath.
2	Negotiate.	Ask yourself, Will I get hurt?	Think: What's the smart thing to do?	Say you're sorry.	Use chance.
3	Tell the person to stop.	Blow out your anger.	Ignore it.	Go do something else.	Swap.
4	Rock, Paper, Scissors.	Make a deal.	Stay and talk it out.	Ask yourself, Will I get in trouble?	Draw straws.
5	Say or think "Stop."	Say what you want.	Take turns.	Stop and cool down.	Share.

SUPPLEMENTARY ACTIVITY #1 GAME CARD #27

<u>S</u>top, <u>T</u>hink, and Pick a <u>P</u>lan Bin<u>go</u>

	S	T	P-	G	O
1	Take a deep breath.	Think: Should I walk away or stay?	**S**top, **T**hink, and Pick a **P**lan.	Apologize.	Get help from someone you trust.
2	Use chance.	Negotiate.	Ask yourself, Will I get hurt?	Think: What's the smart thing to do?	Say you're sorry.
3	Swap.	Tell the person to stop.	Blow out your anger.	Ignore it.	Go do something else.
4	Draw straws.	Rock, Paper, Scissors.	Make a deal.	Stay and talk it out.	Ask yourself, Will I get in trouble?
5	Share.	Say or think "Stop."	Say what you want.	Take turns.	Stop and cool down.

SUPPLEMENTARY ACTIVITY #1 GAME CARD #28

Stop, Think, and Pick a Plan Bingo

	S	T	P-	G	O
1	Get help from someone you trust.	Take a deep breath.	Think: Should I walk away or stay?	Stop, Think, and Pick a Plan.	Apologize.
2	Say you're sorry.	Use chance.	Negotiate.	Ask yourself, Will I get hurt?	Think: What's the smart thing to do?
3	Go do something else.	Swap.	Tell the person to stop.	Blow out your anger.	Ignore it.
4	Ask yourself, Will I get in trouble?	Draw straws.	Rock, Paper, Scissors.	Make a deal.	Stay and talk it out.
5	Stop and cool down.	Share.	Say or think "Stop."	Say what you want.	Take turns.

SUPPLEMENTARY ACTIVITY #1 GAME CARD #29

<u>S</u>top, <u>T</u>hink, and Pick a <u>P</u>lan Bin<u>go</u>

	S	**T**	**P-**	**G**	**O**
1	Apologize.	Get help from someone you trust.	Take a deep breath.	Think: Should I walk away or stay?	**S**top, **T**hink, and Pick a **P**lan.
2	Think: What's the smart thing to do?	Say you're sorry.	Use chance.	Negotiate.	Ask yourself, Will I get hurt?
3	Ignore it.	Go do something else.	Swap.	Tell the person to stop.	Blow out your anger.
4	Stay and talk it out.	Ask yourself, Will I get in trouble?	Draw straws.	Rock, Paper, Scissors.	Make a deal.
5	Take turns.	Stop and cool down.	Share.	Say or think "Stop."	Say what you want.

SUPPLEMENTARY ACTIVITY #1 GAME CARD #30

<u>S</u>top, <u>T</u>hink, and Pick a <u>P</u>lan Bin<u>go</u>

	S	T	P-	G	O
1	Apologize.	Get help from someone you trust.	Take a deep breath.	Negotiate.	Ignore it.
2	Think: What's the smart thing to do?	Think: Should I walk away or stay?	Swap.	Tell the person to stop.	Ask yourself, Will I get hurt?
3	**S**top, **T**hink, and Pick a **P**lan.	Say you're sorry.	Draw straws.	Rock, Paper, Scissors.	Blow out your anger.
4	Stay and talk it out.	Ask yourself, Will I get in trouble?	Say what you want.	Say or think "Stop."	Use chance.
5	Take turns.	Stop and cool down.	Share.	Go do something else.	Make a deal.

SUPPLEMENTARY ACTIVITY #2

STP Match-Up

Match the picture of Scruffy with the STP plan that he is acting out by drawing a line from each picture of Scruffy to the matching STP plan on the left.

Get help from someone you trust.

Go do something else.

Take time to cool down.

Ignore it.

Say what you want.

Make a deal (negotiate).

Use chance.

Say you're sorry.

SUPPLEMENTARY ACTIVITY #3

Stop, Think, and Pick a Plan! Cube Roll

Objective   Students will give examples of behaviors they will use at each STP step.

Materials   Supplementary Activity #3 Teacher Sheet, "STP Cube Pattern"

Procedure   Using Supplementary Activity #3 Teacher Sheet, "STP Cube Pattern," make two STP cubes out of heavy paper. Then divide the classroom into two teams and give each team a cube. The teams will take turns rolling their STP cube. Draw Popsicle sticks with students' names on them to determine the order in which team members will roll their cube.

Each student who rolls the cube should give an example of something he or she would do at the step that is rolled. For instance, if STOP is rolled, a student might say, "Imagine a big red stop sign." If PLAN is rolled, students should give an example of a plan they could use to make a conflict situation better. Since there are so many behaviors at the "pick a plan" step, the word PLAN appears four times on the cube.

Once a behavior is mentioned it cannot be mentioned again. The next person to roll the same step must think of another behavior. While you should encourage students to use the behaviors you have taught them for each step, they may use their own variations at each step as long as these behaviors facilitate an effort to stop, think, or pick a plan.

Each time a student gives a correct behavior his or her team receives a point. If a student cannot think of a behavior or states a behavior that doesn't appropriately fit the step on the cube, then the other team gets a chance to give an example of a behavior for that step. If the team member who answers gives an appropriate behavior, his or her team gets a point. That same team then gets to take its turn at rolling the cube.

Students may begin to complain about there being limited behaviors to cite for a certain step as the game progresses. If that happens, it may be helpful to remind the students that there is a component of luck to this game, as there is in any game involving a roll of dice.

SUPPLEMENTARY ACTIVITY #3 TEACHER SHEET

STP Cube Pattern

Fishing for a Plan

Objective   Students will verbalize real-life situations in which conflict resolution plans they have learned could be applied.

Materials   Supplementary Activity #4 Teacher Sheet #1, "Fish Pattern" (duplicated or traced on various colors of construction paper and cut out)

Supplementary Activity #4 Teacher Sheet #2, "STP Plans" (cut apart and glued to the fish)

Paper clips (to attach to the "nose" of each fish)

Fishing pole (a stick with a piece of string tied to one end and a small magnet tied to the loose end of the string)

Container to hold fish

Two lengths of string (to act as fish stringers—optional)

Procedure   Duplicate or trace the fish pattern (Supplementary Activity #4 Teacher Sheet #1) on different colors of construction paper and ask a student to cut them out. Cut out and glue an STP plan strip (Supplementary Activity #4 Teacher Sheet #2) to each fish. Construct a "fishing pole" (or poles), and fasten a paper clip to each fish's "nose" so the fish can be "caught" by the magnet tied to the end of the fishing line. Allow students to take turns "fishing" in a fish bowl or other "pond," reading the plan on the fish they catch, and giving an appropriate situation in which the plan could be used.

You can divide the fish into several "ponds" so several students can participate at once. Have the students switch ponds after they have "fished out" their pond.

SUPPLEMENTARY ACTIVITY #4 TEACHER SHEET #1

Fish Pattern

SUPPLEMENTARY ACTIVITY #4 TEACHER SHEET #2

STP Plans

Get help so you
won't get hurt

Cool down—
hit a pillow

Use chance—
rhymes

Use chance—
throw a stone into a circle

Go do something else—
find another game to play

Cool down—
draw or doodle

Use chance—
guessing games

Use chance—
draw straws

Cool down—
listen to music

Cool down—
jump on a trampoline

Use chance—
stand on one foot

Use chance—
throw dice

SUPPLEMENTARY ACTIVITY #5

STP Mobile

Objective   Students will review the key components of the STP conflict resolution approach and will construct a mobile that will serve as a reminder of the steps.

Materials   Colored yarn

Dowels, coat hangers, or branches

Tagboard or heavy paper

Crayons or colored markers

Glue

Scissors

Single-hole paper punch

Supplementary Activity #5 Handout #1, "STP Mobile"

Supplementary Activity #5 Handouts #2A-#2D, "STP Mobile Shapes"

Procedure   Lead a discussion to review STP steps to conflict resolution. Tell the students that they are each going to create an STP mobile that will serve as a reminder of the steps for them. Give them Supplementary Activity #5 Handout #1, "STP Mobile," to show them what their finished mobile will look like. Then give them Supplementary Activity #5 Handouts #2A-#2D, "STP Mobile Shapes," and instruct them to color and decorate the shapes on the handouts according to the directions on Handout #2A. After the students have completed coloring and decorating their pieces, have them paste their shapes onto tagboard and cut them out. Alternatively, you could have shapes of tagboard already cut out and instruct students to cut their shapes out and then glue them to the tagboard.

Once pieces have been cut and mounted on tagboard, have the students punch a hole or holes where indicated on each piece. Using lengths of colored yarn they should then hang the shapes as shown on Supplementary Activity #5 Handout #1 to create a multitiered mobile.

STP Mobile

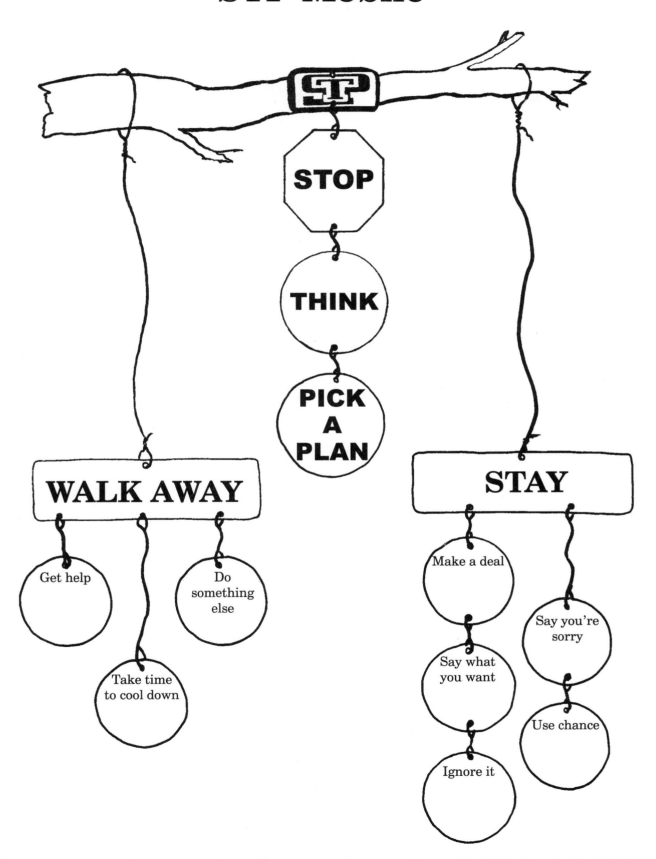

STP Mobile Shapes

1. Color the "STP" shape any color you want.
2. Color the "STOP" shape red.
3. Color the "THINK" shape yellow.
4. Color the "PICK A PLAN," "Walk Away," and "Stay" shapes green.
5. Draw a picture on each of the other plan shapes of someone using that particular plan.

STP Mobile Shapes (continued)

SUPPLEMENTARY ACTIVITY #5 HANDOUT #2c

STP Mobile Shapes (continued)

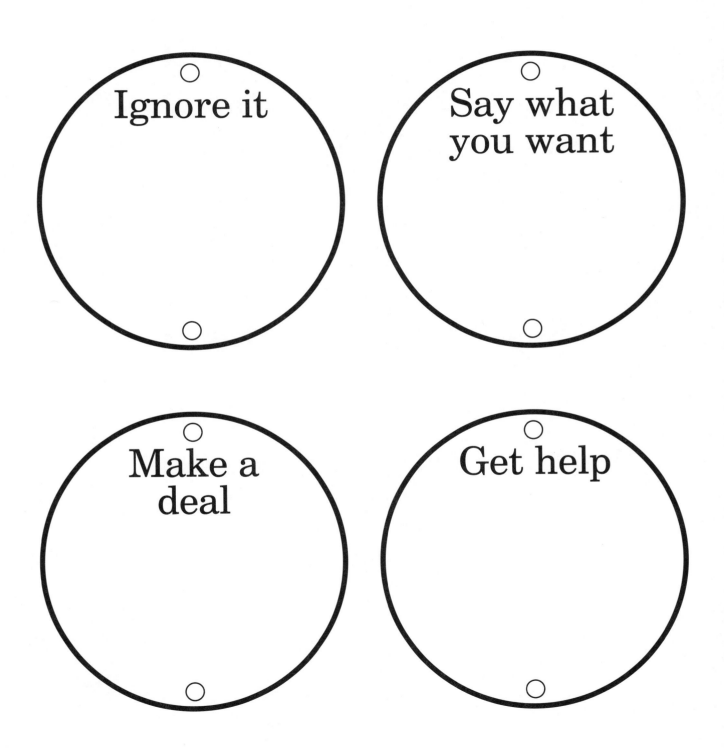

SUPPLEMENTARY ACTIVITY #5 HANDOUT #2D

STP Mobile Shapes (continued)

Lesson 8

How to Handle a Bully

How to Handle a Bully

Objective   Students will learn to apply STP techniques when confronted by a bully.

Materials   Transparency #2 from Lesson 4 – "The Pick a Plan Step (What to Do If You Stay)"

Transparency #1 – "Bullies . . ."

Transparency #2 – "Scruffy's Bully"

Transparency #3 – "Ways to Handle a Bully"

Transparency #4 – "Stand Tall and Don't Act Afraid"

Transparency #5 – "Ignore It and Walk Away"

Transparency #6 – "Tell Them to Stop It and Walk Away"

Transparency #7 – "Stay With Other Kids"

Transparency #8 – "Get Help From an Adult"

Transparency #9 – "Real Bullies . . ."

Transparency #10/Handout #1/Poster #1 – "Bystander Do's and Don'ts"

Transparency #11/Handout #2/Poster #2 – "Bully Do's and Don'ts"

Handout #3/Poster #3 – "Target Do's and Don'ts"

Scruffy the STP Dog puppet from Lesson 1

To the Teacher

Bullying is a widespread and serious school problem. Bullies not only terrorize single victims, they often terrorize entire classes or schools. Multiple studies have shown that repeated exposure to victimization by bullies in the school setting is linked to reduced academic performance, increased apprehension, loneliness and abandonment by peers, chronic absenteeism, lowered self-esteem, and incidents of child suicide. Students who are regularly victimized by bullies carry intense emotions of fear and helplessness with them and have a profound sense of powerlessness, which often lasts into adulthood.

Studies have found that approximately 50% of school-aged children are the victims of bullying behaviors at least once during a given school year. Dan Olweus, an expert on bullying problems, found that one out of every ten students is regularly attacked either verbally or physically by bullies and that elementary-aged students are the most frequent targets. The younger the student the more prone he or she is to be bullied by older students. Bullying can take various forms, ranging from teasing and intimidation to physical assaults and theft of property. Wherever bullying occurs, there is an imbalance in real or perceived power. The bully controls the situation with an intent to inflict injury or discomfort upon the victim.

Bullies generally are kids who feel secure and who have friends, the friends often being children who feel empowered by associating with a bully. While bullies are usually not top students, neither are they failing students. Their achievement level is typically average to slightly below average. Bullies are identified by their personality style. They start their aggressive behaviors at an early age. Most children acquire internal restraints against such aggression early in their development; bullies don't. Studies show that their cognitive makeup is different from that of other children. They have limited feelings of both empathy and guilt, like to be in charge, enjoy the rewards of aggression, and often have a significant role model who has modeled aggression. Bullies have a hostile bias, attributing negative intentions to others and perceiving provocation where it doesn't exist. For instance, if someone accidentally bumps a bully, he or she will see it as a call to fight rather than as an accident. In addition, bullies often seek targets who they feel are ill-equipped to fight back, such as younger and smaller children or students with special needs.

What causes kids to bully others? An inability to cope with difficult situations such as divorce or the death of a relative may cause some children to bully others. Some bullies are victims of emotional or physical abuse. Still others have a strong desire to be the "top dog" and see aggression and violence as a way to achieve popularity and friends.

While bullies are typically thought of as being boys, girls can be bullies also. The aggression of girls, however, takes a different form, being more subtle and complex than the overt actions usually displayed by boys. Whether the bullies are boys or girls, bullying not only causes a great deal of misery for others but it also hurts the bully with negative effects that increase over time. Most bullies experience a downward spiral through life as their aggression negatively impacts their learning, friendships, work, family, mental health, and income. If their behavior isn't modified, bullies often turn into antisocial adults.

Children who are the targets of bullying behaviors have a hard time defending themselves against the attacks. The children chosen as targets of aggressive actions are often more sensitive, cautious, anxious, and quiet than their peers. They display a vulnerability when faced with conflict. Their fearfulness and apparent weakness can set them up for being picked on and dominated by a bully. Victims are often children with few, if any, friends. They have poor self-esteem and may seem depressed, anxious, or moody.

Bullies and their targets have something in common. Research indicates that both groups of children have limited problem-solving abilities and friendship skills. As bullies continue to pick on their targets and as the targets continue to find themselves being bullied, they each develop patterns of response that eventually become part of their personality. It is for this reason that it is important to introduce interventions to address the bullying-target cycle as early as possible. Early intervention can remedy the problem before the behaviors become personality traits.

One way to break the bullying-target cycle is to teach children how to be assertive, rather than passive or aggressive, in their interactions with others. By building students' confidence to handle conflicts and by giving them some strategies to use when confronted with bullying behaviors or seeing others being bullied, students become increasingly able to exude strength and resourcefulness. Bullies become discouraged when the fear, weakness, and passive attitude of targets and onlookers, which encourage bullying behaviors, are replaced by a strong stance.

The philosophy of this lesson is based on the following principles:

- It is important for adults to be involved in helping children deal with bullies because of the power imbalance that exists in bullying situations.

- To stop bullying, a power shift must occur from the bully or bullying groups to the silent majority. Teachers can help this power shift take place by setting clear rules that say that bullying is not allowed and by teaching all students ways to combat bullying behaviors.

- Teachers and other adults must maintain a respectful and nonpunitive attitude in classroom discussions about bullying. Bullies and victims should never be mentioned by name unless a student volunteers that information about herself or himself.

- The primary ways that students learn social concepts are by modeling and discussion. Students should be encouraged to generate their own ideas rather than be given the information through lecture.

- Social skills are best learned as students try out the concepts for themselves. Children can practice what they've learned through role-play, puppet play, and storytelling.

At the end of this lesson, we recommend that you display the posters that reinforce the lesson concepts in a place where students will be able to use them as a reminder for the rest of the week.

Lesson Presentation

INTRODUCTION

Lesson 4,
Transp. #2
Puppet

Throughout this unit we've been talking about how to deal with the types of arguments or fights that all kids run into from time to time. *Show Transparency #2 from Lesson 4, "The Pick a Plan Step (What to Do If You Stay)."* **You've learned eight different things that you can do to solve conflicts. Let's check in with Scruffy to see how things have been going for him since he's learned how to use STP.** *Turn to Scruffy and say:* **Hi, Scruffy. How's it been going?**

Scruffy: **"Rough"** *(said in a low "ruff," barking way).*

Teacher: **What do you mean? The last time I talked to you, you were feeling pretty good about things, especially about working out arguments with other kids.**

Scruffy: **I don't want to talk about it. It'll just get worse if I tell.**

Teacher: **Oh, Scruffy. It sounds like you've run into a bully.**

Scruffy: **How did you know?**

Teacher: **Because you're scared and won't talk about it. That's how people act when they've run into a bully.**

Scruffy: **They do?**

Teacher: **Yes. And lots of kids run into bullies. Class, can you help Scruffy realize he's not alone, that he's not the only one who's had trouble with a bully? Raise your thumb if you've ever been bullied or seen someone else being hurt or threatened by a bully.** *Allow for student response. Draw Scruffy's attention to the thumbs.* **Let's talk about bullies today and what to do if a bully is threatening or hurting you.**

BULLIES: WHAT THEY DO AND WHY

Transp. #1 *Show Transparency #1, "Bullies . . ." and read the comments on the transparency. Then ask students how they would describe a bully. Jot down their comments succinctly on the transparency and then say:* **It's true that bullies are often bigger and stronger and that they do things like trip you, push you, shove you, make fun of you, threaten you, and take your things. But sometimes friends do these things to each other when they're really mad. What makes bullies different is that they like to pick on kids and make kids afraid of them.**

Some bullies do this because they think it makes them look cool. Often, they don't know how to make friends and they think bullying will impress others and make them more popular. Other bullies simply like the feeling of being more powerful or of taking other kids' things. Some bullies are copying things they've seen on TV.

The things bullies do to kids are the things adults wouldn't put up with from anybody. Let's say that your mom was carrying her groceries from the car and someone came along and shoved her down, and took her groceries. What do you think she'd do about this? *Allow for student response.* **Right! She'd get some help, wouldn't she?**

Let's say that every day when your dad walks from his parking space to his place of work a person comes and hits him really hard and tells him if he says anything about this he will beat him up worse. What do you think your dad would do about it? *Allow for student response.* **Right! He'd get help. He might report the person to the police. These are criminal offenses.**

Do you realize that you shouldn't have to put up with things that adults don't put up with? By the end of this lesson you'll know some ways to feel more powerful around a bully, how to have the courage to report a bully, and how to stick up for kids that you see getting bullied.

THINGS YOU CAN DO WHEN YOU RUN INTO A BULLY

Transp. #2

Show Transparency #2, "Scruffy's Bully." **Here's the bully that has been bothering Scruffy. Sometimes he pushes Scruffy down at the bus stop and won't let him sit in the good seats on the bus. Sometimes he gets a bunch of kids to follow Scruffy around and make fun of him on the playground. Sometimes he tells Scruffy he's going to beat him up when no one is around. Let's see if we can think of some ways to help Scruffy learn how to deal with this bully.**

Transp. #3

Show Transparency #3, "Ways to Handle a Bully," covering the two headings, "Might Help Scruffy" and "Might Bring Scruffy More Trouble," with a strip of paper. Ask: **Can anyone suggest some things that Scruffy could do to get this bully off his back?** *Allow for student response. Write the responses on the overhead in the appropriate columns. When the students have finished giving suggestions, uncover the two headings. Read the behaviors listed in the "Might Help Scruffy" column. Explain that these suggestions could help Scruffy handle the bully because they are not actions that would get Scruffy in trouble or make the bully even meaner. Then read the suggestions you have placed in the other column and discuss the possibility of negative consequences from these actions.*

Say: **The experts who have done research on how to stop bullies tell us that there are certain things that will work the best if someone is bullying you. They are to stand tall and not act afraid, to ignore what the bully said or did and then walk away, to tell the bully to stop and then walk away, to stay with other kids, and to get help from an adult. We're going to talk about each of these now.**

Transp. #4

Show Transparency #4, "Stand Tall and Don't Act Afraid." **Kids need to stand up to bullies or the bullying will just get worse. I know that doing this isn't easy. Bullying can make you feel really scared or really sad or really angry. But the bully wants to see you feeling these ways, so you must not show these feelings. To stand tall and not act afraid, sad, or angry takes a lot of courage. You may have to act in a way you don't really feel. But the only smart thing to do is stand tall and look tough.**

Let me show you the difference between acting upset and acting strong. Let's say that a bully on the playground tells me to give him my lunch money. *Ask a student volunteer to play the bully in two different role-plays. Ask the rest of the class to watch the role-plays and observe whether you look strong or afraid. For the first role-play, round your shoulders and hunch them up, lower your head, and look at the ground. Then repeat the role-play, only this time stand up straight and tall and hold your head up. After the second role-play, ask:* **Which time did I look weak? How did it show?** *Allow for students response. Then say,* **That's right! When we're afraid or sad, our shoulders tend to roll forward and our head goes down.**

Which time did I seem more powerful? What did I do that made me look strong and not afraid? *Allow for student response. Then say:* **Yes! By forcing myself to throw my shoulders back, stand tall, hold my head up, and look straight ahead I made myself look like I wasn't afraid. Now I'd like you to practice this. Let's pretend I am a bully to all of you and I tell you I'm going to get you after school. Look weak and afraid first.** *Pause.* **Doesn't that feel awful? Now, hold your head up high and look straight ahead. Pretend you're not afraid. This takes courage and practice, but it's the only way to deal with a bully. You might want to practice in a mirror at home.**

Transp. #5

Show Transparency #5, "Ignore It and Walk Away." **After you've acted like you're not afraid by standing tall and looking straight ahead, another thing you can do is to ignore what the bully did or said and then walk away. You can use the "ignore it" plan from the STP wheel. But remember, ignoring definitely won't work if you look weak or hurt or like you're afraid. Pretend that I'm a bully again. After I threaten you, stand tall and look ahead. Then turn your body as if you are going to walk away.** *Initiate practice.*

When you're getting away from a real bully it helps to pretend that the bully isn't even there. Leave as fast as you can and walk as if you had some place to go.

Transp. #6

Show Transparency #6, "Tell Them to Stop It and Walk Away." **Sometimes you need to do more than just ignore a bully. You need to say something to the bully in a firm, strong voice. If you decide to talk to the bully, give the bully a powerful look straight in his or her eyes. Then say "Stop it" or one of the other things on this transparency. They all really mean the same thing.** *Read the transparency to the students.* **Which of these things would you feel most comfortable saying?** *Allow for student response and tally the responses on the transparency. Tell the students to remember their favorite response so they can use it in practicing standing up to a bully during role-plays at the end of the lesson.*

Ask a student volunteer to represent a bully. Say to the class: **Listen to the power in my voice as I respond to this bully. If I want to make myself look even more powerful, I can put my hand out like this when I say "Stop it."** *During the role-play, model making a powerful "stop" motion with your hand as you say "Stop it." Then ask the students to, again, pretend that you are a bully and practice looking you in the eye, saying "Stop it," and turning as if to walk away. After the students do this once, say:* **It takes courage to make your voice sound strong and powerful rather than afraid or mean. Let's try it again.** *Conduct several more practice role-plays.*

After the practice session say: **You're getting good at this. Don't forget that when you're getting away from a real bully it helps to pretend that the bully isn't even there. Leave as fast as you can and walk as if you had some place to go.**

Transp. #7

Show Transparency #7, "Stay With Other Kids." **Smart kids who don't want to be bothered by bullies make sure that they . . .** *(Ask students to read the title of the transparency.)* **This doesn't mean that the people you are with have to be your friends or even that you have to like one another. It's just safer to stay near others when there's a bully around. Joining in an organized game like kick ball, soccer, or Four Square is how a lot of kids stay safe on the playground. Some kids make it a point to find at least one other kid to hang out with at recess.**

Let's say that a bully tells you he's going to get you after school. How can you stay safe once you're away from school? *Allow for student response. Tell the students:* **Some kids hire a bodyguard. They ask someone stronger or older to protect them and they give that person something in return for his or her help. They may discuss with their parents something nice they could do for the kid who is sticking by their side. Or they may just work out some sort of a deal with the kid that both of them feel is fair. The other thing they do is report the bully to an adult.**

Transp. #8 *Show Transparency #8, "Get Help From an Adult."* **If someone more powerful than you is threatening to hurt you, you need to get some protection. Sometimes another kid will be able to help, but sometimes that won't be enough. Whether you ask another kid to help or not, you need to let an adult know what's going on. No kid should have to live with the fear of getting hurt. Bullies need to be reported and punished. It's not tattling to report a real bully.**

THE DIFFERENCE BETWEEN TATTLING AND REPORTING A BULLY

Transp. #9 *Show Transparency #9, "Real Bullies . . ."* **Let's talk again about what makes a real bully. The thing that is different about bullies is that they like to make kids afraid, pick on kids or hurt them, or take or wreck kids' stuff, and they won't stop when they're asked to. You can tell if you've run into a real bully if you are afraid you'll get hurt and if you can't get the person to leave you alone. If this happens to you, you need report this to an adult.**

Tattling is different from reporting. Most kids who tattle aren't really afraid of the person they are telling on. Their main purpose is to get the person in trouble.

Here's an easy way to tell the difference between tattling and reporting:

- If you're scared a person will hurt you and you can't stop him or her, you've probably run into a bully. You need to tell an adult. That's reporting.

- If you're mad at someone but you're really not in danger and you tell an adult, that's tattling.

Listen to these examples and see if you can tell which are reporting a real bully and which are tattling. If an example demonstrates reporting a real bullying, shout out "reporting." If it demonstrates just trying to get a kid in trouble, shout out "tattling."

1. You see a kid you don't like call another kid a name. You tell an adult.

2. A kid swears at you. You tell an adult.

3. Every day you dread going to school because a kid grabs your backpack and throws it in the garbage can. You tell an adult.

4. The kid beside you is reading a comic book instead of doing his math. You tell an adult.

5. The kids never let you be the captain in kick ball. You tell an adult.

6. A kid tells you to give her your lunch money or she'll tell everybody a secret she knows about your family. You tell an adult.

7. You hate recess because a certain kid gets a crowd of other kids to make fun of the way you walk or run. You tell an adult.

8. You see a kid throwing rocks at a kindergartner. You tell an adult.

9.   **A kid tells you that if you don't do what she says, she'll take all your friends away. You tell an adult.**

10.   **A boy tells you that he and his friend are going to beat you up after school. You tell an adult.**

11.   **You see someone chewing gum. You tell an adult.**

12.   **A mean kid often pushes you and knocks you down. You tell an adult.**

WHAT TO DO IF YOU SEE SOMEONE BEING BULLIED

Transp. #10

Show Transparency #10, "Bystander Do's and Don'ts." **One reason that every school has bullies is that bullies think that no one will report them and that other kids will think they're cool if they're mean. If we want to get rid of bullies in our school, we need to join together. Even bystanders can do a lot to stop bullies. Here are some do's and don'ts for when you see someone being bullied.**

- **DO stick up for the person being bullied by saying things to him or her like: "That was really mean!" or "Don't pay any attention" or "Want to play with me?" OR you could say to the bully: "Leave him alone!" or "That's mean. Stop it!" or "Pick on somebody your own size."**

- **DO offer to go with the person being bullied to report the bully.**

- **DON'T laugh at what the bully says or does.**

- **DON'T just stand there.**

WHAT TO DO IF YOU BULLY KIDS AND WANT TO STOP

Transp. #11

Let's talk about bullies themselves for a second. Let's say that a bully finally realizes that picking on other kids isn't paying off. He sees that it's not making him more popular; in fact, it's just making all the kids not like him. But let's say that he's been a bully for so long that now it's a habit. He's so used to being a bully that it's hard to stop. Let's look at some things a bully could do to

break the habit. *Show Transparency #11, "Bully Do's and Don'ts," and read it to the students. Then tell them that you're going to read it again but you're going to stop now and then and you'd like them to shout out the next word. Point to the word on the transparency that you want them to shout out.*

PRACTICE

**Handout #1
Handout #2
Handout #3**

Standing up to a bully takes a lot of courage, but the more you practice some of the things we've just talked about the easier it will be. Let's practice some more right now. *Divide the students into groups of three and give each group an envelope containing the words "bully," "bystander," and "target." Have each student in each group pull a word out of the envelope and explain that the word indicates the part they are going to play in the first role-play. Tell them that each group will be doing three role-plays, so they will each get a chance to act out each part. Then give each group Handout #1, "Bystander Do's and Don'ts," Handout #2, "Bully Do's and Don'ts," and Handout #3, "Target Do's and Don'ts."*

Explain that you will read what the bully did in a certain situation and the role-play will start at that point . (Take special care to explain that the person who is the bully should not act out the aggressive or bullying behavior.) The bully's job in these role-plays is to stop doing the mean thing he or she was doing and listen to the bystander and the target. The bully can do this by thinking "Stop" and thinking that he or she can be cool without being mean. The target's job is to act like he or she isn't afraid, ignore the bully, or ask for help depending on the situation. The bystander's job is to stick up for the bully and/or offer to go with the person being bullied to report the bully. In the role-play, the bully shouldn't leave the scene until the target and bystander have acted their parts. If the target or bystander is using the strategy of leaving during the role-play, he or she should just turn his or her back on the bully and take two steps. Otherwise kids in different triads might bump into each other.

Use the following role-plays or other scenarios supplied by the students.

- **A kid on the bus threatens to hurt you if you don't give him the dessert your mom packed in your lunch.**

- **A kid on the playground keeps following you around, pointing at your new shirt and laughing.**

- **Every day when you play basketball at recess, an athletic kid makes fun of the way you play. You tell the kid to stop it and the kid says, "I'm just kidding" and keeps teasing you.**

- **A kid tells you she'll get all your friends to not play with you unless you give her the bracelet you're wearing.**

- **You're playing with a puzzle that is a classroom favorite. A kid comes up to you and says he and his friends will get you at recess if you don't let him have the puzzle right now.**

- **An older kid takes your favorite baseball hat on the way home from school and throws it to his friend. They throw it back and forth and tell you to say "good-bye" to your hat.**

- **You are walking to the store to buy something. Some big guys out in front of the store ask you what you're going to buy. You tell them, and they say they want some of that, too. They tell you to hand over your money.**

- **A girl in your class starts playing with your best friend at recess. When you try to join them, the girl says that she and your friend don't like you anymore and that you can't play with them. You're afraid of what the girl will do if you hang around.**

- **Other boys won't let you in the boys' bathroom because they say you are a girl. One boy keeps shouting, "Girl, girl, girl!"**

- **Other girls won't let you in the girls' bathroom because they say you are a boy. One girl keeps shouting, "Boy, boy, boy!" You ask them really nicely to stop saying that, but it only makes it worse.**

- **An older kid on the playground tries to find you every recess. When he does, he tries to trip you so you'll fall down.**

- There's a big kid in your class who walks around during recess trying to find kids who are wearing jackets with hoods. Whenever he finds one, he grabs the hood and swings the kid around. You just got a new jacket with a hood and all of a sudden you see the kid coming toward you.

- Every time you get a chance to go on a swing at recess a girl comes up to you and tells you to get off the swing because she wants it. If you say no she starts to hit you.

- You have a special mechanical pencil that your dad bought for you. You see a really mean kid in your class using it. You tell the kid it's yours but the kid just tells you she *(he)* found it on the floor and it's hers *(his)* now.

LESSON SUMMARY

You've done a terrific job of learning how to deal with bullies! Do you notice how STP and the eight plans work in almost any situation, even with bullies? Think back over what we've talked about today and complete one of these sentences:

- Something in this lesson I'm glad I learned was . . .

- A question I still have is . . .

- A time I might use what I learned today is . . .

- Something I learned today that I'll always remember is . . .

SUPPLEMENTARY ACTIVITIES

Use the supplementary activities that follow this lesson to reinforce the lesson concepts.

- *How Much Courage Does It Take?*
  (Supplementary Activity #1)

- *Star of Courage*
  (Supplementary Activity #2)

- *Get the Picture*
  (Supplementary Activity #3)

TRANSPARENCY #1

Bullies . . .

- Think it's fun to hurt you

- Like to scare kids

- Are often bigger than you

- Try to pick fights

- _____

- _____

- _____

TRANSPARENCY #2

Scruffy's Bully

TRANSPARENCY #3

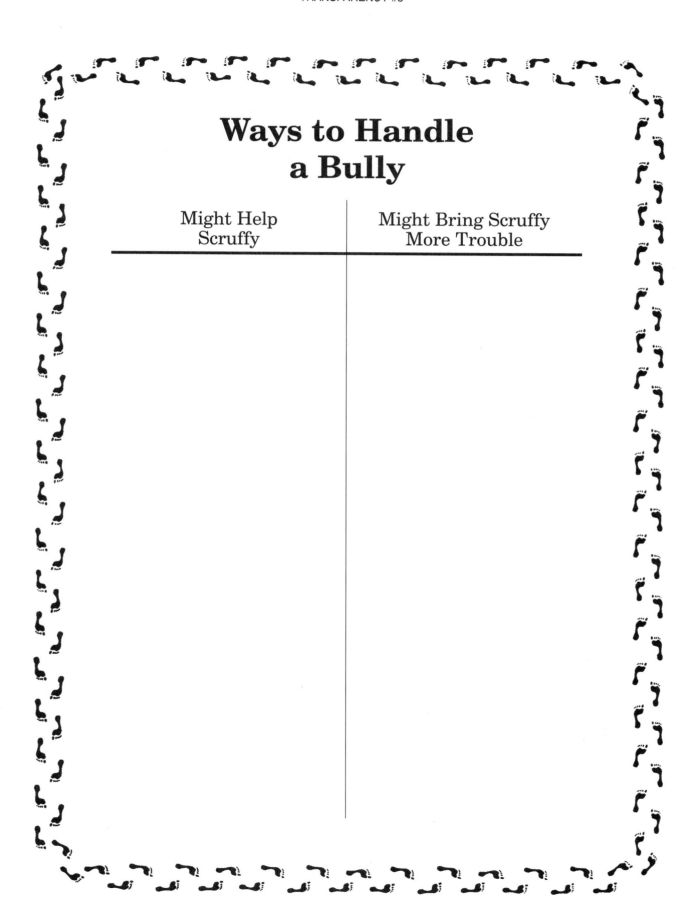

Ways to Handle
a Bully

Might Help Scruffy	Might Bring Scruffy More Trouble

TRANSPARENCY #4

Stand Tall and Don't Act Afraid

TRANSPARENCY #5

Ignore It and Walk Away

TRANSPARENCY #6

Tell Them to Stop It and Walk Away

Stop it.

Stop bugging me.

Cut it out.

Get lost.

Leave me alone.

Knock it off.

I don't have to do that.

I'm going to do something else now.

No Way!

TRANSPARENCY #7

Stay With Other Kids

TRANSPARENCY #8

Get Help From an Adult

TRANSPARENCY #9

Real Bullies . . .

1. Make you feel afraid.

2. Like to pick on you.

3. Take or wreck your stuff.

4. Won't stop when you tell them to.

TRANSPARENCY #10/HANDOUT #1/POSTER #1

Bystander
Do's and Don'ts

Do's:

1. Stick up for the person being bullied.

   For example, you could say to him or her:
   - "That was really mean!"
   - "Don't pay any attention."
   - "Want to play with me?"

   OR

   You could say to the bully:
   - "Leave him (her) alone!"
   - "That's mean. Stop it!"
   - "Pick on somebody your own size."

2. Offer to go with the person being bullied to report the bully.

Don'ts:

1. Don't laugh at what the bully says or does.

2. Don't just stand there.

TRANSPARENCY #11/HANDOUT #2/POSTER #2

Bully
Do's and Don'ts

Do's:

1. Say "stop" to yourself.

2. Tell yourself, "I can be cool without being mean."

3. Go find something else to do.

Don'ts:

1. Don't pick on other kids.

2. When you're mad about something, don't take your anger out on other kids.

3. Don't threaten to hurt other kids.

HANDOUT #3/POSTER #3

Target
Do's and Don'ts

Do's:

1. Act like you're not afraid. Stand up straight and look the bully in the eye.

2. Ignore what the bully said or did or tell the bully to stop in a way that sounds powerful. Then walk away.

3. Ask for help from an adult.

Don'ts:

1. Don't show you're afraid.

2. Don't talk in a weak voice.

3. Don't let a bully see you cry.

How Much Courage Does It Take?

Objective Students will evaluate the different degrees of courage needed to respond to various bullying situations.

Materials Supplementary Activity #1 Handout, "How Much Courage Does It Take?"

Procedure Read through each of the bullying scenarios on the handout with the class. After reading each one have the students write down the degree of courage they think it would take to intervene in the manner described. Explain that they should use a scale of 1-3, with 1 being the least amount of courage needed and 3 being the most. After the students have completed the handout, discuss their ratings by asking the following questions:

1. Which situations do you think would take the most courage?

2. In which situation would it be easiest to stand up to a bully?

3. What's the most courageous thing you've ever seen someone else do or done yourself when faced with a bully?

4. In situations in which it's hard to stand up to a bully, what would be some things that might make it easier for you to have courage?

5. What is it about a bully that makes him or her seem so powerful?

SUPPLEMENTARY ACTIVITY #1 HANDOUT

How Much Courage Does It Take?

1. **Read** each item below.
2. **Decide** how much courage it would take to do what the item says.
3. **Write** down how much courage it would take on each line.

1 = a little courage   **2 = an average** amount of courage
3 = a lot of courage

_____ 1. A classmate you don't usually play with is being bullied. Go up to that person and ask if he or she wants to join in a game you are playing.

_____ 2. Tell a bully to stop picking on your best friend.

_____ 3. Ignore a bully who teases you.

_____ 4. Tell a bully to stop picking on a kid who doesn't have many friends.

_____ 5. Stand up to a bully who is your age and is picking on a younger kid.

_____ 6. Tell your teacher or the adult on playground duty about someone who is bullying you.

_____ 7. Tell your teacher or the adult on playground duty about someone who is bullying another kid.

_____ 8. Walk away from a bully and get help.

_____ 9. Tell your parents or another relative about a bully who is bothering you.

_____ 10. Act unafraid and strong when a bully picks on you.

_____ 11. Tell a bully to stop picking on you.

Star of Courage

It takes courage to handle a bully. From the list below, cut out the things you think you'd really do when faced with a bully and paste them in the points of the star on Handout #2. Then write your name on the line in the center of the star.

Get help	Ignore what the bully said or did
Walk away	Don't act afraid
Offer to go with someone being bullied to get help	Say, "That was really mean"
Stay with other kids	Tell the bully to stop
Say, "Leave him (or her) alone"	Look the bully straight in the eye

SUPPLEMENTARY ACTIVITY #2 HANDOUT #2

Star of Courage

SUPPLEMENTARY ACTIVITY #3

Get the Picture

Objective   Students will come up with and illustrate responses to bullying that
bystanders can use.

Materials   Supplementary Activity #3 Handout, "Get the Picture"
Crayons, markers, or colored pencils

Procedure   Give students Supplementary Activity #3 Handout, "Get the Picture."
Read the first frame of the cartoon aloud to the class and point out the
courage it would take to be a bystander and help out the mouse being bullied. Ask the students to draw in the second frame what happens next,
showing a bystander doing or saying something positive to help the mouse
being bullied. When the students have finished their drawings, have them
share their cartoon ideas with the rest of the class. Discuss their ideas, af-
firming the importance of bystanders and the positive ways that bystanders
can intervene.

SUPPLEMENTARY ACTIVITY #3 HANDOUT

Get the Picture

1. **Read** the first frame of the cartoon below.
2. In the second frame, **draw** what happens next, showing a bystander doing or saying something positive to help the mouse being bullied.

Appendices

Appendix A
A Schoolwide Approach to Conflict Resolution

Appendix B
The ASSIST Program Scope and Sequence

Appendix A
A Schoolwide Approach to Conflict Resolution

The Stop, Think, and Pick a Plan (STP) approach is most successful when it is implemented on a schoolwide basis. If your school decides to use this conflict resolution approach, everyone on the staff, including administrators, educational assistants, custodians, regular parent volunteers, secretaries, specialists, and all teachers, should be introduced to the STP process. Research shows that when all adults consistently have the same expectations and use the same terminology to help students handle conflicts appropriately, there's a marked increase in student success in this area. Consistency is the key. Staff members who don't participate often find themselves sought out by students who want to tattle, complain, or get attention.

A schoolwide approach to managing conflicts establishes a sense of school community and contributes to a peaceful school in which the majority of students consistently demonstrate respect for themselves, others, and school property.

The first step in building a schoolwide approach is to establish a "site-based team" that is representative of the entire school staff and includes the school administrator. The team members determine the best ways to implement the STP approach in their particular school setting. It may be possible to use an already existing committee such as the school's Discipline Committee. One member should be appointed to facilitate group process and ensure follow-through of goals and ideas.

The following are some strategies that have been used by school site-based teams to get everyone on board and working toward a consistent, schoolwide approach to resolving conflicts.

1. Provide inservice training for classified and certified staff on the STP process and on how to coach students through it.

2. Make sure all staff and supervisors of students use the same procedures for breaking up fights and resolving conflicts by providing them with prompt sheets using STP terminology.

3. Teach staff to use "teachable moments." See "How to Use This Curriculum" in the front of this manual for the fundamentals and basic steps of this powerful strategy.

4. As a team, brainstorm ideas for reinforcing STP implementation and dealing constructively with staff resistance. (See #7 below.)

5. Arrange for schoolwide lessons for the student body. Clarify who will do the teaching, if co-teaching will be done, and what the timeline should be for mastery of the STP concepts and internalization of conflict-management behaviors.

6. Consider what could be done at school assemblies to help students gain a working knowledge of STP principles and procedures. Some school staff, aware of the effectiveness of humor, have developed assembly programs in which staff members play the part of students at their best and worst moments. They gain student attention through the hilarity of the skit and then slip in the STP self-management concepts.

7. Implement schoolwide reinforcement ideas:

   - Place STP posters in strategic places.

   - Create bulletin board displays that illustrate the STP concepts.

   - Use the intercom to sustain the STP process throughout the school year by (1) reading the reinforcement tickets that model good self-management skills, (2) reading examples of conflicts over the intercom that classrooms can solve, (3) asking students to perform a specific STP behavior for the day, and (4) reading "thoughts for the day" in the area of conflict resolution.

   - Awards/tickets/reinforcers

   - Each month, tally the number of students referred to the office for discipline by grade level or classroom and place the totals in the weekly staff bulletin. Teachers can share this information with their students, comparing the number of discipline referrals to that for the previous month (the second year the referrals can be compared to the same month the previous year) and having the students brainstorm ways to lower the number of discipline referrals for the coming month.

   - Utilize parent links. Use the parent newsletter or other means to solicit parent help in reinforcing the lesson concepts.

   - Focus posters, assemblies, and classroom lessons on ways to resolve cross-cultural disputes to increase tolerance for and appreciation of cultural differences.

Appendix B
The ASSIST Program Scope and Sequence

Kindergarten	Grade 1	Grade 2	Grade 3	Grade 4	Grades 5–6
Teaching Friendship Skills: Primary Version – Recommended list of children's books	***Teaching Friendship Skills: Primary Version*** – Lessons 1-3 – Appendix A: Using Literature to Enhance Students' Understanding of Friendship	***Teaching Friendship Skills: Primary Version*** – Lessons 4-8 – Appendix B: Friendship Games	***Teaching Cooperation Skills*** – Lessons 1-7	***Teaching Friendship Skills: Intermediate Version*** – Lessons 1-7 – Appendix A: Multiple Intelligences Friendship Center – Appendix B: Using Literature to Enhance Students' Understanding of Friendship – Appendix C: Friendship Games	***Helping Kids Handle Conflict: Intermediate Version*** – Lessons 1-15
Building Self-Esteem in the Classroom: Primary Version – Recommended list of children's books – Lesson 1 and Kindergarten Workbook	***Building Self-Esteem in the Classroom: Primary Version*** – Lessons 1-6 – Student Workbook (First Grade)	***Helping Kids Find Their Strengths*** – Lessons 1-7 (Primary)	***Building Self-Esteem in the Classroom: Intermediate Version*** – Lessons 1-3 – Student Workbook (Intermediate)	***Helping Kids Find Their Strengths*** – Lessons 1-9 (Intermediate)	***Building Self-Esteem in the Classroom: Intermediate Version*** – Lessons 4-9 – Self-Esteem Activities for Older or More Capable Students (Unit Five)
	Helping Kids Handle Conflict: Primary Version – Lessons 1-3	***Helping Kids Handle Conflict: Primary Version*** – Lessons 4-6	***Helping Kids Handle Conflict: Primary Version*** – Lessons 7-8	***Helping Kids Handle Conflict: Primary Version*** – Lessons 10-15	***Multiple Intelligences*** <u>***Helping Kids Handle Conflict***</u> – Lessons 10-15